Jellied Eels and Zeppelins

'I have just retired from teaching art to a group of elderly folk,' she informed us. At the time she must have been about eighty, but...

She lived in a large detached house not far from the town. Nothing had changed since I was there thirty years previously. The murky kitchen still had a deep earthenware butler sink and wooden draining board, no 'fridge'. The dark oak panelled dining room and chintz covered chairs in the sitting room were as I remembered them, no television. Isabel shared the house with her sister Mary and friend Rose. She suffered from the painful condition trigeminal neuralgia, causing acute pain to the side of her face. Mary, the housekeeper, cooked and cleaned. Recently, although in her eighties she had been climbing a tree to pick some apples when the poor dear had fallen and broken her back. She was in constant pain. Rose, a lifelong friend, had lived with them for about fifty years. The chauffeur of the trio, she drove the elderly car with difficulty; also considerably dangerously! She had severe torticollis, which left her head dramatically turned to the right. Isabel sat in the passenger seat and gave her directions and instructions. These three devout elderly ladies led a very cloistered life.

That evening we shared a memorable meal with them in their over-ornate dining room. Mary, unable to sit with a fractured spine, reclined on a chaise longue. Isabel could not bite or chew her food so mashed it to a pulp and sucked it. Rose was quite expert at aiming her food around the corner to her mouth, but sometimes missed. The whole scene could have been sad

JELLIED EELS AND ZEPPELINS

WITNESS TO A VANISHED AGE

Sue Taylor

Copyright © Sue Taylor, 2003

First published in Great Britain 2003
by Thorogood

Published in Large Print 2004 by ISIS Publishing Ltd,
7 Centremead, Osney Mead, Oxford OX2 0ES
by arrangement with Thorogood

British Library Cataloguing in Publication Data
Taylor, Sue
    Jellied eels and Zeppelins: witness to a vanished age.
    Large print ed. – (Isis reminiscence series)
    1. Elvin, Ethel May 2. Large type books
    3. Great Britain – Social life and customs –
    20th century 4. Great Britain – Biography
    I. Title II. Elvin, Ethel May
    941'.082'092

ISBN 0–7531–9946–7 (hb)
ISBN 0–7531–9947–5 (pb)

Printed and bound by Antony Rowe, Chippenham

For Mum, Dad and Ethel

ACKNOWLEDGEMENTS

Writing this book was never going to be easy. I mean, how do you cram more than 90 years of someone's life into the pages of a book? Ethel's recollections are countless. However, we had to stop somewhere and had it not been for the help of the following people, compiling the book would have certainly proved more difficult:

BBC Essex, Angie and my mother-in-law, Dorothy (known as Dot), for first putting me in contact with Ethel; and Dot also for her knowledge of the East End and the Second World War; my family and friends for all their support, especially Hayley and Gaynor for their computer skills; Ethel's friends, relatives and neighbours for looking after her so well, especially Rosemary, who often made notes when Ethel remembered something in my absence; staff at the London Borough of Waltham Council and at the Vestry House Museum for assisting with my enquiries; all at Thorogood (especially Angela), and at Acorn Magazines (especially Pippa); and last, but by no means least, Ethel herself, for her kindness, sense of humour and friendship, and for making my visits so enjoyable. Thank you, Ethel, for sharing your memories.

Sue Taylor

FOREWORD

In the summer of 1999, Ethel May Elvin was sitting in her cosy kitchen listening to the radio. She had it tuned to BBC Essex when an elderly lady phoned in to talk about life during the 20th century. Ethel was then in her 90th year, older than the caller and yearning to relate her own experiences. Indeed, friends and relatives had often encouraged her to write her memoirs, but with poor eyesight (she had cataracts at the time, but has since had them removed) and arthritis in her hands and legs (caused, she believes "by sitting in the dugouts during the Blitz with me feet in water!"), she realised that she needed some help. So, with the assistance of the BBC Essex Helpline and my attentive mother-in-law and her friend Angie who had been listening, I was put in contact with Ethel and recorded the first of many interviews on 17th August 1999. The resultant six articles were published in the Essex Magazine in 2001.

Since our first meeting, I have come not only to admire, respect and be amazed by Ethel's remarkable memory, but to regard her as a special friend and a truly inspirational character.

That Ethel survived at all — considering the fact that she was a child of "delicate health" and escaped the dreaded "Spanish Flu" pandemic of 1918/1919 as well as both World Wars, including the London Blitz, is a feat in itself. That she should have come out of it with such an amazing capacity to laugh — even now that she is housebound for most of the time — is incredible.

This book is one woman's journey through life in the 20th century from Walthamstow E17, where she was at first her father's unwanted daughter, to Doddinghurst village, just a few miles north of Brentwood, Essex, where she and her husband, Joe, made the bricks to build their own house. There might not be many miles between the two places, but there are certainly many memories during this long journey. "Jellied Eels and Zeppelins" is a tribute to all those who helped Ethel on her way. I feel immensely privileged to have worked on it. Not only have I got to know a most remarkable lady, but I have been able to gain an invaluable first-hand insight into what life was like for ordinary working-class families from the beginning of the 1900s.

But Ethel isn't "ordinary" — not really, not by today's standards. She, and many others of her generation, showed — and still do — immense courage, fortitude and spirit, not only when it was needed, but throughout their lives.

This is Ethel's story, told mostly in her own words with respect and devotion, sorrow and acceptance, humour and tenacity. It's in her words, because it's better that way.

Some of the names of the people in this book have been changed to protect their right to privacy.

Sue Taylor

Contents

Part One

1909–1923

used for cottage, always kept in a glass jar. A few years before retirement in 1993 the building was demolished. The Education Department replaced it with an ordinary rectangular demountable building. I felt really sad at the end of an era.

One year the fire engine arrived on its annual visit to be greeted by excited children. The tall handsome fireman who talked to the children said delightedly, "Do you know when I was five I used to sit on Mrs Day's lap".

It gives me great pleasure to see the children grow up to be successful. One very bright girl predictably became a doctor, another very quiet, rather shy child is now one of our local historians. She has also formed

Rare very occasionally one can predict a child who will not be a success in life. One such boy, it was very difficult to get, was always one of the challenging children. He tried to bury his pen to teacher instead of cutting

16

CHAPTER
ONE

Chocolates and Shoe Leather

"I was born at Cassiobury Road, Walthamstow, on 16th November 1909, to Edwin and Florence Turner, and was of such delicate health that my mother received an extra four shillings a week from the War Office for me.

When I had a bath, Mum said that I made her feel sick, I was so skinny. My sister, Florrie, was the fat one. She had a podgy face and she used to play with the kids in the garden. She was the king of the kids at our school, she used to be the boss, 'cos she was the eldest.

Cousin Flo's mum brought me into the world. Dad wouldn't look at me 'til I was a year old. Uncle Charlie — Dad's eldest brother — lived downstairs and Mum and Dad lived upstairs, and he came home from work and came up to my Mum in bed and said "What yer got?" Mum said "Another girl." Uncle Charlie said "What's Ted got to say about that?" My mum said "He won't even look at 'er." Charlie said "Miserable ol' so-and-so!" Mother said that Dad was so mad that she'd had another girl that he stomped into the kitchen and the china fell off the dresser and made me nervous.

I had a touch of what they called St. Vitus's Dance over it when I was a baby.

You know what Uncle Charlie did? We 'ad four brass knobs on the bedpost. He went out and bought me a pair of little mittens and a pair of socks and stuck 'em on each of the knobs and said "There you are, you poor little soul. If your father won't buy you anything, then I will!"

In about 1916, Mum miscarried a boy. I think I was about six. Dad put me down all the same . . . But I remember that Cousin Flo's brother, Herbert, when he was born, he was that tiny, you could have put him in a pint jug. My Dad wanted to adopt him when Aunt Flo died and my uncle said "No, you're not going to have my son just 'cos you can't have one of your own!" And I remember that so clearly. My Dad wanted to adopt him and that stuck in my mind. Funny isn't it?"

Ethel believes that her father's wish for a son in an age when men did most of the manual work, was why he taught her how to "mend shoes, hang wallpaper and bang in nails. It was always me who had to help 'im, never Florrie."

Ethel remembers helping her father mend their shoes: "It was the first time he called me Jane. I was only about six or seven. I never questioned him and, after that, he always called me Jane and I never knew why."

Edwin's way, like many others of his generation, was never to show affection: "He never kissed me once and I never kissed him. He showed Florrie more affection than me. And yet, when he was ill in hospital towards the end of his life, he turned to me and said 'You've been a good daughter to me'. But I did have great respect for my father. I always did as I was told. The only time I ever answered him back was when I was 24 and broke up with a chap that he liked. Florrie argued with him a bit, but not me. We never held much conversation with Dad. He just used to tell you what you had to do. 'Jane!!' he used to shout in his booming voice. When I looked after him in his later years, when he was being stubborn, he said once 'Don't you talk to me like that, you're my daughter!' I said 'Yes, and I'm an old age pensioner too!!'

"He had a voice that boomed 'cos of his time in the army during the First World War, when he told the men what to do. He frightened the life out of me when he shouted. I only had to look in his icy blue eyes and I was gone. He had that Sergeant Major look, I used to call it, and that was enough. I never used to stop and argue. I knew better than that. He didn't believe in hitting kiddies though."

One particular occasion that Ethel remembers well, was when her elder sister, Florrie had been misbehaving all day: "Mum told her to go along to the local hardware store, to buy a cane. The first time Florrie returned with a bundle of wood for lighting the fire. Mum sent her back again. This time, naughty Florrie had bought candles, so Mum ordered her to return to the shop. On the third occasion, my sister had bought the cane and Mum hung it over the line above the fireplace, telling her that if she misbehaved again, she'd get the cane across her legs. When Dad came

5

home and saw it, he was furious. He grabbed it and whacked it behind Mum's ankles telling her sternly: 'Does that hurt? Now you know what it feels like. Don't ever let me see you hitting those children!' Then he broke the cane in half and threw it away.

'That was the only time I ever saw him hit my Mum. He didn't believe in hitting women. He reckoned it was disgusting. But he done that on her legs to prove to her how much it hurt — what it felt like. She weren't allowed to smack us, but my sister used to say, when my mum gave her a wallop now and again, 'cos she was a little devil, 'I'll tell Dad!'

"Dad was a complex character. He never saw us kids go without anything. He was good — we never had no luxuries, just the bare things. My Dad always used to provide us with food, clothing and shoe leather. He made sure we never had wet feet and that there was food in our bellies. That's what I mean when I say he was a good dad. He brought us up well, I must say that. We never had no luxuries of any sort — no sweets or anything, only when he started working at Lonco, then we used to get his free samples."

Edwin also insisted on good manners at the dinner table. "We used to have to sit with our elbows in plates for one hour if we were caught with them on the table." *The children were also never allowed to ask for anything — they had to wait to be offered.*

Working as a parcel delivery man for Lipton's-owned Lonco, Mr Turner would sometimes bring home sweet samples. On one occasion, he had with him a small box of chocolates: "Father offered us one each. He then

6

offered Florrie another but not me. The next day when he was out, I decided to help myself to a chocolate. In the evening, we went to a relative's for tea. Just before we sat down, Father told us all to be quiet. He said that we had a thief among us — someone had stolen one of his chocolates. Well, I realised that he knew it was me, so I shot under the table and that's where I stayed for the rest of the evening!"

Naturally, the feeling that Florrie was her father's favourite caused many problems between the two girls and there were the inevitable fights: "I used to have lots of little bruises where Florrie pinched me in the bed we shared."

Ethel's sister also once hit her with a stick because she refused to do the washing up when it wasn't her turn.

Another fracas occurred one Sunday afternoon, when their father asked the two girls to go to Pops, the local publican: "You used to get allowed so much beer free and, as we had a relation of ours coming from Blackfriars, my Dad said to my sister and me 'Take these two pint bottles up to Pops and get them filled up with beer' . . . Well, this day — it was a Sunday afternoon — we had a pint bottle each to carry up Coppermill Lane to get them filled up. We were halfway up the road, near the school, when my sister said 'You can take the two bottles and bring them back!' I thought 'Why should I?' so I put my bottle on the floor and said 'I'm not taking it!' She said 'You pick that up or I'll give you one!' So I picked it up and knocked her on the head with it! It was a glass bottle and she went crying all the way down the road to tell Mum and Dad. I followed her. They told me to take the two bottles back up the road and get them both filled up with beer. You always get what's coming to you."

Ethel's father also liked to keep up appearances when the family went out together as he was a very proud man: "My Dad used to take us round to relations of ours just for a little walk when we came back from Sunday School. We used to have a cup of tea and then come back for our dinner. Dad used to walk behind us and say 'Hold your shoulders up, walk in line with the pavement!' He used to pull our shoulders back if we didn't do it. We used to get away with it a little bit with my mother, but not with my Dad. He made sure that we kept our feet straight, so that we didn't get pigeon-toed. 'Look at yourself in the shop window!' he used to say. And, after that, we used to look in the shop windows, even when we were out on our own.

Dad wouldn't let us read the newspapers, but, when Emily Davison threw herself in front of the King's horse at the Derby in 1913, Dad showed us the paper. He said 'See that. That's the sort of thing that happens when you try and control something.' (I think what he meant by 'control' you see, was that they was trying to control the Government). He reckoned that it was clever. He agreed with women getting the vote. He reckoned it was fair for the woman with the position she had in a man's house, to have the vote as well. He really believed in it."

An Act in 1918 allowed women of 30 and over, married to a property owner, or property owners themselves, to vote in elections. It wasn't until 1928 that there was full equality, when all women over 21 were given the vote.

"Mum was quite thrilled to be able to vote. I'll tell you what my Mum used to do — I remember seeing her do it when I was a kid. She and her women friends, 'cos they were in the Labour Movement too, used to pull our Labour MP's cart up the road with him sitting in it! His name was Valentine La Touche McEntee and he was a lovely man, very helpful. You could go and talk to him. Mum was very, very keen to get the vote and never missed the chance to.

"The first time I voted, I remember saying how proud I was. It was a funny feeling, when I think of it. I felt very grown up.

"Some of the women were very oppressed in my day and age, especially when a lot of men were knocking them about as they used to. A lot of it went on behind closed doors. My Dad didn't beat up my mother. He didn't smack us either. He didn't believe in it."

CHAPTER TWO

Busbies, Prawns and Bing, Bing, Bing!

"My Dad was born in May 1884 and my Mum in April of the same year. Dad was the youngest of six, three boys and three girls, but the girls all died within three weeks of each other from diphtheria or scarlet fever when my father was two years old and his mother went on the drink. She came from Ireland. My grandfather used to go looking for her . . . she used to leave my Dad outside the pub. Then she suddenly disappeared and left him with three boys. That's why my Dad wouldn't often touch none of it (*drink*)."

Edwin's mother was eventually tracked down to Bethnal Green, but it was left to his wheelwright father, Charlie, and his cousin, Polly from Maldon, to raise the three boys: "The one I used to call Gran, or Aunt Polly, was a cousin of my grandfather's. She lived at Maldon and she'd just lost her husband. She was only a young woman and she came to look after the boys. Aunt Polly used to cook for my grandfather. My Mum used to say 'You've got two grans,' and I could never understand why. Aunt Polly — oh, she was really lovely, the sweetest old lady you could ever wish to meet, she was."

Edwin Turner joined the army aged 17 during the Boer War, though he never saw active service: "He used to wear a big hat on sideways — like they did in the Boer War. He also wore a busby and that was when it was real fur. It made a dent on Dad's nose, 'cos it was so heavy. He stood on guard when Queen Victoria died and he said that they had to stand still for four hours then. He said that the soldiers dropped down like ninepins and they weren't allowed to touch 'em — they had to leave them there. But my Dad stood rock still the whole time."

Edwin first met Ethel's mother, Florence or Floss as she was known, when they were at school together. Floss, the youngest of four children, was raised by her older sister, Alma, when their mother was admitted into a sanatorium after her son died from a brain disorder aged just two.

"My Mum had brown eyes and lovely long black hair. I was told that her father was foreign and that he looked Spanish. He had curly black hair, a curly moustache and curly sideboards. When she was 17, my mother worked as a barmaid in the East End, often working until two in the morning. She couldn't keep her flat going and, as she had to start work at five in the morning, she slept in a bath at the pub. Dad took her away and married her to stop her from getting tuberculosis! (*The couple married in 1905*).

"My Dad very rarely drank, but when he did, he'd only have two pints and it made him happy, 'cos he wasn't used to it. He came home from work one day and he was supposed to have come home mid afternoon on Saturdays for Mum to have been able to go shopping. This was just after the first war when he used to drive around London, taking stuff to the docks. He met a lot of friends from his old firm and he went out with them and didn't come back 'til 10. We were all sitting round, we'd just had a cup of cocoa, I'll never forget it as long as I live. Mum couldn't get any groceries, 'cos she didn't have no money and the next day was Sunday. There was my sister and her friend Edie and me and another friend of hers, I was about 14 then, I think, and Dad came in. He always used to hang his coat on the kitchen door and, as my Mum took the cups out into the kitchenette to wash them up, she said 'There's something wrong with your father — sounds as if he's wobbling.'

Dad came into the room, took out a brown paper bag and put it on the table. 'I've brought you some prawns,' he said to my Mum. She came in and said 'You're drunk.' 'No, I'm not,' said Dad in a slurred voice. Mum said 'There's something wrong with you. There's me waiting for some money to go and get some food and tomorrow's Sunday — there won't be any shops open.' 'Oh,' he said and, as he was hanging his coat up, Mum got the tablecloth and — I've never forgotten it — we had this big black range you know, and she shook the tablecloth in the range with the prawn bag on it and then she went back out into the kitchenette with the rest of the cups!

Dad turned around and said 'Where's my prawns?' Mum called out 'In the grate where they should be!' My mother was very placid, but when you put her out, you knew about it. She went to the sink — she had the whole of the tea service in there — and began throwing its contents. They went 'Bing, bing, bing!' He was dodgin' 'em and they was comin' through the door and whizzin' by me and do you know, when I looked at his face, he was gasping, he couldn't believe it. She said 'I'll keep you waiting for grub. I've no food in the place, so there'll be no dinner tomorrow and you girls go to bed!' Edie whizzed out of the door like a bomb and the other one. We went to our bedroom and shut the door, 'cos it frightened us a bit, you know. We never heard another sound, so we put our bedclothes over our heads and went to sleep. How the argument finished, we never knew, but next day, Mum gave us some toast — she never gave my Dad anything, never even made him a cup of tea. None of us had any dinner that Sunday. On Monday, when Dad came home, he'd bought a new tea service for my mother! I remember, it was cream with green leaves on it."

CHAPTER THREE

Inkwells, Laundry and Doh-Ray-Me

"I went to school when I was five. Coppermill Lane Infants School was the first one. You went to the infants' school, then the juniors, and then you went to the big girls' school. It was all in one massive building down one side of the street and then you had the big boys' school on their own. At the bottom of the sandy path there had been a copper mill years and years ago, that's why it was called Coppermill Lane.

"When I had just started at the infants' school at the top of the road — my Mum's sister-in-law (my Aunt Florence, who had brought me into the world), she took me to school that morning. Before she got back home, I had run back, run away from school. My aunt took me back again, and I ran away again. The third time she returned me to school, I had to stay. I didn't like the kids looking at me — being a new kid, I suppose that's what it was. I was a shy person.

"I was about ten or eleven when I went into the big girls' school. I couldn't go to the high school, 'cos Mum couldn't afford the uniform. But I wasn't all that clever and I couldn't picture meself in that uniform — it was green and yellow.

"I hated arithmetic. I was wonderful at sewing though — more practical than academic — but, at school, if anyone laughed at my stitches, I hated it.

"We didn't have no uniform while we was there. We just wore a skirt and blouse or a dress. You had to be smart and clean. They used to look at your shoes, look at your fingernails, everything, you know. Dad always used to make us polish our shoes every morning before we went to school. If we forgot, he would soon find out!

"Miss Muffet was a lovely teacher. She was a governess, actually. She was our head teacher. And we had a head teacher of the juniors and one for the infants, you see. Girls and boys were mixed in the infants and juniors.

"They had a big hall and all the doors leading to different rooms were off this hall. For one subject, you went into one classroom and for another subject, you came out and went into a different classroom. We always used to be in the hall for morning prayers. Then we dispersed to our rooms. One teacher, Miss Wilmer, used to teach singing. She had a long stick and used to say 'Doh-Ray-Me' and, if you went out of tune, she would say 'Come out here!' and the ol' cane used to reach across and pull you out.

"When I got to big girls' school, the girls used to have one day a fortnight laundry and one day a fortnight cookery. I think that the boys were taught carving, woodwork and all that. They used to alternate it every week. We went to a different school for that. It was the William Morris School for cookery and Chapel End School for laundry. When we had cookery lessons, my Mum used to give me a mug with cocoa and sugar in it and say "When it comes to your break time, you can ask them to fill it up with hot water and make you a drink." I used to keep the mug under me desk, and keep dipping me finger in it, so by the time it was break, it had all gone!

"Meat pies, cakes — I enjoyed that. They would give you a demonstration in a little room and, if you cooked it all right, they let you take it home and we often did. They gave you all the ingredients and they showed you how to do it and, if you wanted it, they would sell it to you. We didn't have to pay a lot of money, roughly sixpence.

"We were also taught how to light a fire, how to do our ironing and all that. How to do the washing — it was good. We had a lovely sewing class. They reckoned I was a good sewer. I used to do a lot of sewing — my stitches were very good.

"We were taught reading and writing, the ABC, but no story writing, nothing like that. We were taught how to add-up, times-tables and that sort of thing. I used to like geography. They used to give us a lot of geography — about foreign countries, different wars and how they lived. I used to like history too.

"We had a service every morning, when we went into the hall. We had prayers and Miss Muffet used to pick out the hymn. My favourite hymn was 'All Things Bright and Beautiful' — I used to love that.

There must have been about 25 to 30 in a class. We didn't have it overcrowded. We used to write with pencil mostly. We wrote with ink if we had any compositions to do. One or two summers, they took us out of the school up to Richmond Park (*recreation ground*), up the end of Coppermill Lane, where I lived. By the reservoir there, it took you out to Richmond Park and the next day, you had to write a composition about what leaves you saw, what colours they were, what their names were — about nature, you know. We never went out on no coaches, just walking. We couldn't afford a coach-ride then. We took ourselves.

"Once a month, we could go to the swimming pool, if we wanted to. We had to walk two miles for that. But my Mum wouldn't let us go, 'cos it meant that as we came out and had to walk home, our hair would be all wet and we might catch cold.

"School started at 9 o'clock in the morning, 'til 12, then you could go home 'til 2 o'clock and lessons ended at 4. During the morning break, my mother used to come along if it was cold, with a hot cup of cocoa or soup. She would give it to us through the railings to Florrie and me. A lot of the mothers used to do that. The majority of children used to go home for their dinner (not lunch) at dinnertime. They never did meals at the school then, not like they do now. We never sat down for a meal at school. We never had no homework either.

"Miss Simpkins was one of our teachers and Miss Osborne — I didn't like her. Miss Harvey was lovely. One of the girls I was at school with, she was always in trouble. She was always having the cane, 'cos if you done anything wrong, you went to Miss Muffet and, if she thought you deserved it, you got the cane and your name went in a book. It was one Monday morning and all the inkwells were filled up — they used to fill them up every Monday morning. We were all sitting in the class and this Miss Harvey always used to wear a lovely coloured blouse, pink or blue, and she would hold onto the back of this old-fashioned Windsor chair and talk to you. I remember, this particular morning, she said something and this girl answered her back, so the teacher said 'Come out here!' Before she did, this girl picked up one of these inkwells and threw it at Miss Harvey, right in the middle of her lovely pink blouse. All the ink ran down it, so Miss Harvey said 'That's the cane for you again!' That girl was always getting the cane. Right across the legs, it was. They only got a couple of lashes, but Miss Muffet didn't used to hit them hard. I never got it, My Dad used to say 'Don't you ever come home here if you get the cane!' And I never did get the cane."

Indeed, it seems that Ethel was a model pupil, always on time — "Dad wouldn't allow us to be late anywhere and I never am now."

Miss Muffet, wrote her last school report, dated December 20th, 1923, of which Ethel is justifiably proud, for it states: "Regular and punctual in attendance. Clean and tidy, polite and a neat worker."

"We used to have to go to Sunday School. My Dad made us go until we left school and went to work. Then I didn't bother so much. I used to think about enjoying

18

myself then. We had to wear our one set of best clothes and change when we got back.

"For one hour on a Sunday afternoon, I taught the Catechism to about 12 children aged eight to twelve. Two years I did it at St. Oswald's, Walthamstow. I was 14 when I stopped. I used to love it. I wouldn't say that I was all that religious, but I believed in it quite a lot."

CHAPTER
FOUR

Cockles, Carts and Motor Cars

Occasionally, after school in the summer, Ethel's mother would take her daughters on outings to Southend-on-Sea: "We left school at 4 o'clock and we used to get ready and Mum would take us to Blackhorse Road station to go to Southend. About 25 minutes roughly, the journey took on the train. Mum, Florrie and me used to walk right down the Front, where that big hotel is down the slope, and we used to sit on the Front there and get an ice cream. It was just a trip — lovely though.

"We always came back for tea. Mum couldn't afford to buy us tea there. Perhaps we might buy rock or something. My sister sometimes had some cockles, but I didn't, I didn't like them. Under the pier there was a family business called Going, I think, which sold dinners, cockles and all that. We used to have a cup of tea and a slice of toast or something like that. If Mum could afford it, 'cos they were quite dear, she might have some jellied eels.

"You never had a lot of money to spare. One shilling and three-pence, I think the fare was to Southend for an adult. I was about eleven or twelve then. We used to go about two or three times in the summer. When she could save enough money she would take us. When she hadn't got quite enough, she'd take it out of our money boxes (she always paid us back though). It was mostly on a Monday when we went. Dad used to pay her on a Saturday, and, if she'd got a few coppers over, she used to save it and take us to Southend. We were never back late, 'cos we used to have to be in bed by 8 o'clock.

"We had one holiday to Southend, when we were children and Dad had come out of the forces at the end of the First World War. We stayed near the old gas works in a bed and breakfast, but we came home after two nights, 'cos the place was full of bugs."

In the early 1900s, there were only a few thousand private motor cars in Britain. However, by 1914, this figure had increased dramatically. Although Ethel's father later drove a Lipton's delivery van, he did not acquire his own car until the early 1930s: "It was an Austin Seven and we went to visit Florrie in it after she was married. Mum was not allowed to ride in the back, in case the body broke in half!"

When Ethel was very young, her father drove a horse and cart for work: "Dad used to work for London Parcel Delivery and he had a horse there — he used to love his horses; he always used to have the light-grey ones. He used to come home at dinnertime and have a meal and always used to take me up and down the road sitting on the horse's back. Florrie didn't like horses, but I loved 'em.

"Mum would send me out with a bucket and a shovel whenever a horse went by. Cousin Flo told me that they used to call it 'pringling' — picking up the horse manure for the garden.

"On one occasion, when Dad was doing his deliveries, he went back to his cart only to find a black dog eating some meat that he'd pinched out of one of the parcels. Dad didn't dare touch him in case he got bitten. The dog came every day after that for Dad to give him his lump of meat. Another time, he jumped off the back of the cart, ran into a butcher's shop and grabbed some beef!

"Dad named him Jack and eventually took him home with him. Jack once chased off a burglar over the back fence. Dad finally lost the dog when he was chased off himself by the butler at one of the houses he delivered to!

"I remember the trams — they had a pole and seats on top. They used to pull the pole down and put it on the other line and go the other way. If you got in the way, you'd feel it all right! When it was pouring with rain, when you went upstairs, all the seats were wet, so we used to take an old cloth in our pockets to wipe the seats before we sat down, 'cos there were puddles on them.

"My Mum used to walk everywhere, so did my sister and I, so did Dad. The road where I lived was all gritty sandy stuff. I used to love it when the old water carts came down. I asked 'Mum, can I hear the water carts?'

and she would take me out and stand me at the side of the road and I loved all the water that used to splash on you and the smell when the water was going on the hot sand — it was lovely. I can see it now: the cart with all the pipes at the back spraying the gravel. When it was hot, the sand shifted, so they used to water it to keep it down."

CHAPTER
FIVE

Jellied Eels and Christmas Time

When she was still a baby, Ethel's family moved from Cassiobury Road to Glenthorne Road, Walthamstow. They lived there for a short time before moving again to Edward Road. Of their downstairs flat in Edward Road, Walthamstow, Ethel says: "We didn't have a bathroom, only an outside toilet for eight: four from the upstairs flat and us four from downstairs. There used to be a bit of a queue if anyone was in the toilet for very long! The twins, Alice and Mary, who lived upstairs, were a year older than me, so I had all their cast-offs.

"We had a copper in our little kitchenette and we used to boil that up for the bungalow bath. Once a week we did that for our bath on a Friday night. We called it Amami Night, 'cos we used Amami shampoo. Most people did. Our flat was lit by oil lamps. There was a tap in the kitchenette and a big black range. We could only have a roast dinner in the winter when we had a coal fire. We had an oil stove for cooking and a Primus stove. We used to boil all the kettles on the Primus or the oil

24

stove for the washing and the washing-up. When Mum did a very big wash, she used to boil up the copper in the other little room where the sink was.

"My Mum used to blacklead the range. It had one oven and by it was a plate. We had an old tabby tom-cat which used to sit on the plate by the oven and, when it turned round, I used to have to put its tail out! It used to catch alight!

"That was when you could buy cats' food on a stick. In the market was a shop and they used to sell it. There was a big glass case in the window with a horse carcass in it for cats' food. You got three lumps of meat on a skewer. You had to order it and they used to bring it round and stick it through your letter-box. It cost a penny. I always remember that. The cats used to love it — the raw horse-meat. They used to know when it was coming round and would grab it as they put it in the letter-box. Funny, that was. We used to call our cat Tommy. I can still see that cat.

"We had a dog called Laddie at one time too. He was an elk-hound and used to worship our family, especially us girls. When Dad shut him out of the home and wouldn't feed him for 24 hours, 'cos he bit him, it broke our hearts. He gave him water and he didn't hit the dog, just shut him out.

"On Fridays, Mum used to go along to the fishmonger's to buy a cod's head. She would boil it up to make a jelly, which she would strain to remove the bones. We would then spread it on our bread and eat it. It used to be lovely.

"After cooking tea for us when we came home from school, Mum would treat herself every other Friday to fish 'n' chips from Methven's fish shop. They cost threepence and she was known as Mrs Threepence because of that.

"She used to go up to the market on a Friday, shopping. Once a fortnight she would have jellies (jellied eels) and mash for sixpence from Manze's Eel and Pie Shop and the next Friday, she would go to the fish shop . . . so she had a variation. That was her dinner. My Cousin Flo always knew when she had jellied eels. She used to say 'Aunt Flo — you've got a bit on yer blouse' ('cos Mum was a stout woman in her chest, you know). She always used to catch Mum going down the High Street. 'I know where you've been Aunt!' she would say.

"Mum loved jellied eels. Dad didn't and I couldn't eat eels if you gave me a shilling . . . yet they're marvellously good for you. Cousin Flo used to love 'em. She always had them when she went down to the seaside.

"Joe (*Ethel's husband*) used to go and catch eels at Walton-on-the-Naze, when he went to visit his friend in his cottage. He brought a big one home one day and it slipped down the sink and out into the drain and he caught it. His brother used to love 'em. I remember at the beginning of the Second World War, I saw some live eels in Manze's, so I went in and said 'I'd like a couple of those for my mother-in-law, 'cos she's got a bad leg.' But the shop assistant gave them to me all wriggling. I said 'I can't take them like that, can't you chop 'em up?' But he didn't, so I sat on the bus with the paper bag screwed up tight at the top in case they got out in the bus!

"Another thing we used to have at home when I was a girl: we used to take a jug into the butcher's shop and get it filled with pease-puddin' and faggots — used to be lovely. That was only about threepence or something, ever so cheap. And we used to dip our fingers in the pease-puddin' and, by the time we got home, it used to be nearly all gone! We used to eat it goin' along. That was in the market again.

"Mum used to make gorgeous soups for us — that's what kept us going. She would burn some sugar on a spoon and stir it into the soup to thicken and brown it. I also liked Edwards Desiccated Soups. Mum would also make some delicious stews in a huge cast iron cooking pot, which would be simmering on the stove for two days. She would make them with the two penn'orth of pieces (oddments of meat) that she bought on most Saturday nights after 10 o'clock from the butcher's; she sometimes used to use bacon rind and pearl barley too. We couldn't afford to waste a thing — 'Waste Not, Want Not' was the motto of the time.

"We used to go up to Parade Bakery in St. James' Street, Walthamstow, for bread sometimes two or three times a week. They weighed every loaf that came off the counter and if it was under weight, they used to give you what they called a "makeweight" — that's a piece of cake or bread that was kept on the side. They would cut off a piece to make the weight up. Mum used to say

'Don't eat the makeweight!' but, by the time we got out onto Coppermill Lane, my sister and I had eaten it, 'cos it was nice and fresh. 'Have you eaten the makeweight?' Mum would ask. And we would say 'No, Mum' and she used to laugh and say 'No, I know you didn't!' But she knew we had, 'cos we always did. Sometimes, you used to have a nice big bit. (*Makeweights were also used when buying other commodities like beer and ice cream*).

"And I can also remember 'The Toffee Shop', where they used to make their own cough candy twist and peppermint rock, and you could buy a slab of toffee — separate toffees were more expensive. You could buy Milk Tray loose too — I bought Mum a quarter once for her birthday.

"Before the First World War, when we were quite young, it was Florrie's and my job to make up the fire on Christmas morning with newspaper, coal and wood, which Dad used to put in our stockings. As for presents, sometimes we just got an orange, but one year, Florrie and I received a stuffed rag doll. On another occasion, when our father was working for Lonco when I was about nine (after World War I), Florrie got a solid chocolate lion and I got a chocolate elephant — they were delicious. Dad used to say 'Your Christmas dinner is your gift.' He would say that later to Florrie and her husband, Alf, too when they came to dinner.

"We never had a Christmas tree, but hung up paper chains that we'd made ourselves. For Christmas dinner, we'd eat a cockerel or have a joint of beef if we were lucky. We used to go to a pantomime at the Walthamstow Palace of Varieties, towards the top of the High Street. They used to have lovely pantomimes. We would sit 'up in the Gods' and throw our apple cores down whenever there was any cheering. We never went to any Old Time Music Hall — we couldn't afford it — though Mum used to talk about stars such as Nellie Wallace, Marie Lloyd and Vesta Tilley.

"I loved to go to the market at Christmas time. Mum used to take us when I was about six or seven. I remember seeing the stalls all lit by gas lamps and helping a dwarf shake papers off the oranges on the fruit and veg stall. He used to earn himself some money by helping out. Loveable fella, he was. He had an extra large head, which he said he wanted to sell for research when he died. I believe that he did."

Ethel remembers Marks and Spencer in its early days (the company was founded in 1887): "When you went into the shop, it was all open in the front, no proper shop-front or anything. There were counters all the way round and it was called Penny Bazaar.

That's how Marks and Spencer started. You used to walk in and pick up anything, and everything was a penny; elastic, everything.

"As you walked into a wide front — it used to go narrow at the top — there were all tiles, and then, in the middle . . . there was . . . as big as my table . . . all done in different coloured tiles . . . an old fashioned penny. That was Marks and Spencer when I was a little tot.

"My Dad worked at Lipton's for donkeys' years before the First World War. He used to do parcel deliveries. He used to sit in the kitchen with Tommy Lipton and have a meal. They used to treat him very well. I remember that Dad used to go up to Old Street Station, London, to pick up his van. Then he used to go to the East India Docks mostly, to load up. He would grumble about the dockers. They packed up at 4 o'clock in the afternoon. He used to have to line-up in the queue. Sometimes, when he got to the front to be loaded, they packed up and went home and he would have to wait until the next day. He used to wait for two hours sometimes. Mum would say 'Your Dad's come home in a bad mood, be careful what you say!' He would leave home at 6 o'clock in the morning. He used to be up at 5 o'clock and he often used to work part-time in the evenings too when we were very young."

CHAPTER
SIX

Zeppelins, Dolls and Spanish Flu

The Great War of 1914-18 was the first in which civilians were threatened with the fear of air raids. Ethel was just six when she saw the hydrogen-filled airship, the Zeppelin: "I can still see that Zeppelin. It was massive and I'll never forget the droning it made. I remember seeing an airship coming down in flames at Cuffley, Hertfordshire — even though it was miles away, it lit up the sky. I was about five or six then and was holding Dad's hand when I saw it coming down.

"We was all together when another Zeppelin, came over. Cousin Flo, she was very comical. She had a loud voice and she used to take-off Nellie Wallace, an old music-hall star. She used to have a flower in her hat and she used to dance, Nellie Wallace did. A woman at the biscuit stall in the market used to take her off too — singing and dancing.

"Flo was just turned 14 then and she said 'Come on you kids, I'm going to dance for you.' And she pulled out the kitchen table and stood on it and took-off Nellie Wallace and made us kids laugh, to take our minds off it. Afterwards, I remember opening her bag and saying 'What have you got in there, Flo?' and she gave us all a doughnut to keep us quiet!

"Mum and Dad never actually told us that we were at war. We never had no radios or anything like that and Dad wouldn't let us read the newspapers."

On June 28th 1914, the Austrian Crown Prince, Archduke Franz Ferdinand, and his wife, Princess Sophia, were assassinated by a Serb while visiting the Bosnian capital, Sarajevo. This was the spark that ignited the conflict leading to World War I.

"My Mum told me about the Archduke and his wife being shot and Dad thought that there would be a war."

At the start of World War I, Britain's army consisted solely of volunteers. When the government realised that the war was not going to end quickly, a massive recruitment campaign took place, led by Lord Kitchener.

Ethel's father, Edwin, rejoined the army in 1916 after having left to work at Lipton's shortly after he married. "Dad didn't mind being called up, because he said 'Someone has got to fight this war,' and I think that he rather liked army life."

Ethel still possesses Edwin's Army Service Corps (ASC) badges and "The Soldiers' Pocket Testament" he was given with its inscription reading:

"I pray that God's
Blessing may rest
On the Reader and
The Reading of this
Little book. November 1914."

"I've also got my father's baton, which he used when he was a military policeman stationed in Guernsey. It has a leather strap and grooves on the handle, so your hand doesn't slip. Once he caught three Irish soldiers escaping from barracks after curfew. There was a struggle and Dad hit one of them with his baton. The soldier had to go to hospital, but Dad got away with cuts and bruises."

Edwin's duties also included bringing horses over by boat from Weymouth to the Channel Island, where he and his colleagues trained them before they were shipped off to France to take part in the war. The horses were used to drag equipment and supplies including artillery to the front-line and records show that, by the end of the war, more than eight million horses had been killed in the conflict.

"The horses came over with red tapes in their tails. Dad used to go and sit with them, 'cos the crossing was so rough. He said that some of them used to jump about a lot because they got frightened when the sea was rough, especially when the boats passed through The Casquets, where the tides met. It was always very choppy there and the horses used to get sick. I remember Dad telling me that he used to come out on deck sometimes, to get a bit of fresh air and then went back down again for fear of getting washed overboard. He had the horses on the island for so many months, then the officers used to come over and get 'em and they'd be taken off to France.

"Dad really had a way with animals and he especially loved horses. He told me 'Never hit a horse, 'cos they always remember.'

"Dad and his mates also used to keep watch on the Channel for anything unusual. They were away from the fighting."

During his spare-time, Edwin and his friends used to sit on the rocks and wait for the ormer tide to come in bringing with it the ormers — edible abalones (marine snails), also called sea-ears, which have flattened, oval-shaped shells with respiratory holes and a mother-of-pearl lining, and are used as a food in the Channel Islands.

"Dad was a very good swimmer and diver and he and his friends used to dive into the water before the shellfish stuck themselves onto the rocks and then they wouldn't have been able to get them off. The shellfish were like oysters, but with knobbly bits on the outside. They had mother-of-pearl inside and Dad brought us all the shells back. They were different sizes and the fish were delicious when fried.

"He also used to buy lots of tomatoes and grapes from St. Peter Port (*Guernsey's capital*) and bring them home for us kids and there were these large biscuits, which looked like dogs' biscuits, but they tasted lovely too.

"I was about six or seven when Dad has his affair. When he used to come home on leave during the war, he would go straight round to this woman's and my Mum found out. She went round there and said 'You ought to be ashamed of yourself — you've got a husband fighting on the front-line and you're taking my husband away!' I think it only lasted for three or four months, but I did lose a certain amount of respect for my father over it. I couldn't help it. My mother was a good wife to him, she was. She thought the world of my Dad. She looked after us kids ever so well too and never took a day off. And that's all the thanks that she got.

"On the huge field called The Elms at the back of our flat in Walthamstow, where we used to go and pick up the tennis balls for a penny, there were specially erected tents where they made mustard gas bombs. My Dad came home on leave once and Florrie and I had just come home from school. Dad asked 'Where's your mother?' and Florrie replied 'On The Elms making bombs!' Dad said 'Right — I'll make a bomb!' and he went and dragged her out, shouting 'You're not making those sorts of things and you're not leaving those two kids! I didn't marry you to go off to work. Get home and look after the girls!'

"A lady up the road took the job and Mum looked after her two children, so she had the four of us and did her little bit that way."

With no television or radio to follow the events of the Great War, British families either had to scan the newspapers or watch the Pathé News at the cinema:

"We always used to go on a Friday night. It used to cost threepence to watch the Pathé. My sister and I, when we was younger, we used to go to the Saturday morning pictures — that cost a penny. We would get a comic or an orange when we came out. They always cut the film off at the most exciting part to make sure that you went back the next week. The Carlton Cinema was a lovely cinema opposite the Walthamstow Palace. There was the Sarsaparilla Stall outside, where when we was older, we used to have a glass of sarsaparilla before we went in. St. James Street Cinema was a flea pit. It was known as 'The Jameos' and you used to see serials there. We used to pay for ourselves to get into the cinema — a penny. My Dad gave us our 'Saturday penny' for washing and drying-up and for cleaning the knives and forks on an emery board. And that penny, or the penny we were given by anyone who came to visit, was split by Dad into two ha'pennies or four farthings.

"We had two money boxes like pillar boxes on our mantelpiece marked 'F' for Florrie and 'E' for Ethel. We used to put a ha'penny in there every Saturday, but, if we went to the pictures, we'd use the whole penny. With the two farthings we had, we'd get two lots of sweets. Two we saved and two we could spend. Sometimes Mum borrowed our money, but she would always pay us back. I can see her now putting a knife in the slot of the box to get the pennies out. 'Look girls,' she would say afterwards, 'I'm putting it back!'

"When I was two and a half, Mum took me into the post office. I put my hands on the counter and I could just see over the top. She gave me a book just like a pension book and it had 12 spaces in it. Mum said 'Each one of those spaces is a penny — when you've got a bookful, you've saved one shilling. That's your savings book.' I saved from when I was two and a half to when I got married and I spent it all on my wedding and on some of the furniture, the curtains, lino, the lot — it even paid for my car to the church. My chap hadn't got it, so I paid it."

The King and Queen during the First World War were George V — who succeeded to the throne on the death of Edward VII in 1910 — and Queen Mary, whom he had married in 1893.

"He was very nice, but she was a domineering woman. Queen Mary always seemed very stuck-up and strait-laced. She always had one of those hats on her head and she used to walk with a parasol. The King would do as he was told and always did the right thing.

"Gran (Aunt Polly) and Grandad (paternal) were the caretakers of a big old house in Bramham Gardens, Earls Court, before and for a while during the First World War. It was a big five-storey house — I can see it now — and Gran and Grandfather lived in the basement. Gran was the cook and Grandfather was the butler. I can remember going down into the kitchen looking for Grandfather once. There was an iron spiral staircase at one end. Grandad was sitting at the top playing 'The Merry Widow' on this brass thing like a bicycle wheel, like a hurdy-gurdy. That song has stuck in my mind ever since.

"Grandfather's nickname for me was 'Pins and Needles', because he said that I could never sit down for five minutes (I think it was because of the St. Vitus's Dance I had when I was a baby!).

"Us children weren't allowed to go upstairs, only when requested by the family. We used to have to curtsey. Gran caught me going upstairs once without permission and she told me off. Right at the very top of the house was the nursery. Gran took me upstairs once and I remember seeing all these dolls in glass cases all the way round.

"It really was like that television programme, 'Upstairs Downstairs.' Downstairs there were six bells along the kitchen wall and an electric light up in the ceiling. When they wanted to see anything at close range, they used to pull it down on a pulley, right onto the table, so they could see what they were doing. There was a big butler sink too — it was very posh. Gran used to buy pigs' chitterlings (*the smaller intestines of pigs*), put them in salt water, clean 'em and fill 'em with sausage meat and cook 'em for the downstairs' staff. They were lovely. There was also a real sunken garden full of fuchsias with another big garden further on.

"The German Baron and his family, who owned the house, also owned another at Littlehampton. Grandfather used to stay there for a couple of days to clean the windows and tend to the garden there.

"My sister, Cousin Flo and Cousin Charlie were allowed to stay with Gran and Grandad, but I wasn't — I suppose I was too young. I was about two years old, when Gran had them for about a week. They were all dressed up — I remember my sister walking up these steps to the front door of the house, with this lovely red outfit on: a red hat with white fur on it and a red coat; and Charlie had a new suit. I stood by the gate, holding my Mum's hand, watching them.

"I did join them once for a few hours when I must have been about four. It must have been on a Sunday and Gran had bought us girls new hats to go to church in. They were like straw panama hats with white ribbons on the front. Gran had a parrot named Dolly and Charlie was tormenting her. Dolly got so flustered that she tipped her seed all over the floor. As I bent down to pick up the seed, the parrot pecked a big hole in my new hat!

"When war broke out, the Baron had to leave the house, though Gran and Grandad stayed on for a while to sort out the family's belongings. The family gave my sister a doll . . . a German doll, beautiful it was. It was dressed in a blue crepe dress and I can see it now — there was a red ring with a red stone on one of the doll's fingers, red earrings and a red bracelet, beautiful black curls, a little cloak, a hat and shoes. They used to make lovely faces on dolls years ago, the Germans — natural, beautiful, they were. I was really envious, 'cos I didn't get one. They also gave us a pram with a long china handle and a green cover. My sister used to put her doll in it and wouldn't allow me to push it."

The doll was eventually passed down to Florrie's great granddaughter and when Ethel happened to spot it in her bedroom on a visit, she told the little girl the doll's story: "The dress had faded from its original colour to a pale lavender, but its face was still beautiful. They were astounded that I'd remembered it.

"The German Baron didn't come back to Bramham Gardens, so he said 'sell the house,' so the house was sold and Gran and Grandad went and worked at Philbeach Gardens in the same area, Earls Court."

Although rationing during World War I was not as extensive as it was during World War II, food shortages were experienced throughout Britain, especially after the bad harvests of 1916.

"I can remember lining up for potatoes for what seemed like hours, my sister and I, outside Giddens, the greengrocer's, at about eight in the morning. They were brothers and had a shop at either end of the street. Florrie stood at one end and me at the other. When one of us had to go to school, Mum took her place in the queue. Sometimes, she would try to dodge in, so that she would get two lots, one for us and one for Mrs Dawson next door. I think they used to allow us about two pounds each of potatoes. We used to have the old swedes after that.

"There was a family living opposite us. Their name was Vesey. The mother was German and the father Turkish. They were the nicest people you could ever wish to meet — a lovely, beautiful family. There were six children, two girls and four boys . . . all teenagers they were. Well, when the war started, those boys went overseas and fought their German cousins. One of the sons got injured and, when he returned home, became a cinema operator.

"After the war, when the old soldiers used to come round the streets singing for a few coppers, the mother would never let them pass without giving them money.

And she would take them indoors and give them a cup of tea."

During the First World War, rioting occurred in many areas where German families were living. A German pork butcher named Muckenfuss was one of those affected: "Another German was a butcher in out market. I remember holding my Mum's hand when I was about six years old. We was going shopping in St. James Street during the First World War. There was a lot of shouting going on in the street. Mum said 'Come on, we'll get away from here.' I saw many people around the butcher's shop. Some of the men then went upstairs to the flat and threw the piano out of the window. I remember it coming down and, just before it crashed onto the pavement, my Mum pulled me away. I think he moved away after that."

It was estimated that the Great War claimed 10 million lives. But in 1918, the year it ended, doctors were claiming that the so-called "Spanish Flu" was killing even more people worldwide.

"Aunt Flo, when she was carrying again, she died of it and Cousin Flo caught it as well. She was very ill and we thought we were going to lose her too. My Mum went round there and nursed her, so my sister stood on a box and I stood on a stool, and we put a big tub on another box and we did the washing while Mum was looking after Flo and the others. And, when she got better, my Mum caught it and my sister and I nursed our mother.

"Cousin Flo lost every hair on her head and wouldn't go to work, cos' she'd got a bald head and

Mum — she told me this herself — mixed old-fashioned brilliantine with paraffin and rubbed it in Flo's head every day. She said 'I've got Flo's hair growing!'

"We used to call Flo Fanny Nine Hairs! She went to work with a frilly mop hat that Mum made for her out of shantung (*heavy Chinese silk*). My Mum saved her life.

"Isn't it funny when we look back and remember all those things? Flo did have lovely black hair before she lost it and it grew back all curly. And her brother Charlie was curly."

The First World War ended at 11 o'clock on the morning of 11th November 1918, and there was great rejoicing, but also enormous sadness for all the bereaved: "My Mum picked us up out of bed and she said 'Come on, you two, you'd better get up, the siren's going.' Then she said 'It's all right, it's the all clear!' We had just come to the end of the war. It was a Saturday morning.

"I remember the Peace Teas with all the trestle tabled down the middle of the road. And we had a platform and people were singing and dancing and doing turns. Florrie and I were dressed as Japanese girls. We had paper chrysanthemums in our hair that Mum had made. I was sitting there, watching it all, and my Dad tapped me on the shoulder and said 'I'm home!' He'd been demobbed. I remember the first suit he had. He want up to the market and had it made with the ticket or whatever they gave him. And the first day he went out in it, it rained and the suit shrunk and the trousers came up to here. And he said 'Look at this damn fine suit they give yer!'

"After the War, Dad was offered a position in the prison service as a guard, but Mum didn't want us girls to have to live near a prison — the job would have come with a house, you see. He was two inches too short anyway. I used to see him swinging from the door-frame to try and make himself taller. It didn't make no difference." *So Edwin Turner went back to work for Lipton's.*

Part Two

1923–1939

CHAPTER
SEVEN

Hats, Coats
and Cameras

Ethel left school at 14 to earn a full-time wage, though she and Florrie had worked part-time in a sweet shop: "Dad came in once and caught us scrubbing the floor. 'You're not doing that at your age — OUT!' he said. The manager of the shop had once asked me to clean his shoes too, but I told him 'I'm not here to clean your boots!'

"I left school on the Friday and on Monday, Florrie and I had an interview at Houghton-Butcher manufacturing Co. Ltd. (*The company merged to become Houghtons and Butchers in 1926. In 1930, the firm came under the sales umbrella name of Ensign, a camera manufacturing company in Walthamstow.*) We started at dinnertime on the same day. Florrie had left school before me as she was older, and had been working as a dressmaker, which is what my father wanted me to do. But she was no good at it, so she left and we both got work at Ensign.

"When my sister started work two years before me, Dad bought her a coat — 'Cos he said that she should have one to go to work in. When I left school to start work, I wanted a coat. Dad agreed to buy me one. We went up to our local drapery shop, Lidstone's — they had two big shops — and Mum and Dad bought me a coat. It was chocolate brown with fur around the collar and cuffs.

On the second Friday I got paid. Mum took my wage packet, put it on the table and said 'You'll open that when your father gets in'. Dad came home from work and saw that I'd got eight shillings. He give my mother seven for my keep and he said 'Here's shilling for you.' I thought that was really good, but then he said 'Ah — wait a minute!' He split the shilling into two sixpences. Now this is what my father done. He give me sixpence and said 'This sixpence, you can have to spend. The other one, you can pay to me every week until you've paid me 25 shilling and a shilling extra for borrowing the money for your coat!' Yet he gave my sister hers. My mother never forgave my father for that. You know what he said when I'd paid it up? 'That'll teach you not to borrow money!'

"It was a good lesson, 'cos I never 'ave done — only the three pounds I borrowed from him for our bed when I got married. He said then 'You can borrow it on condition that you pay it back with your first week's wages when you go back to work.' And I did.

Florrie worked as an 'engraver', stencilling the company's name onto the cameras. She was at Ensign until her marriage in 1927. I later became a 'tester' or inspector, a chargehand, supervising about a dozen female workers, and worked there for 18 years.

"When I was laid off for a few months, when they was a bit slack, I worked in this toy place. I got it on me own. Down the market it was. Well, what happened, I'd been there a fortnight. I was on the big power press (they'd found out that I'd used a hand press at Houghton-Butchers, so they put me on the power press. Great big heavy thing, it was).

"I started at eight in the morning and worked 'til 12, then I used to rush down the market and have some dinner and come back at half past one and carry on 'til half past five. I was working on these big sheets of metal — bodies for these toy cars — and I went round to get some more metal and to go to the toilet (you had to ask the forelady for the key to the toilet door and you were only allowed to go twice in the morning. You got told off if you went more than twice). I came back and they'd oiled my machine and mucked about with it, so the pedal was rather low on the floor. I put my foot on the pedal and slipped, so I put out me hand to save meself and squashed me finger on the press. They stopped the press than and sent me home on me own. I was really in pain and remember walking down the market and around Woolworths and they was watching me in case I passed out.

"I got down Coppermill Lane and, when I reached home, Mum said 'What you doin' home?' I told her that I'd hurt meself. Florrie was still in bed, so Mum said 'Come on, Florrie, we've got to get Ethel to hospital.' My sister got up, took one look at me and passed out! So I said 'She's not much good to me, I'll go to hospital on me own.' I went to Connaught

Hospital and they gave me five stitches in my finger. After that, I wouldn't go back to the toy company, so I returned to Houghton-Butcher and they said that I could start in the inspections department. I really loved that job and enjoyed going to work.

"Dad used to wear a flat cap for work and a trilby for going out. Mum used to like to wear hats too. When I was a kid, I would say to my Mum 'You've always got second-hand things. You've never got no new clothes. When I grow up, I'll get you something new.' When I started work, I had that on my mind. It took me quite a long while to save £5, 'cos I was only getting eight shillings a week 'til I was 21 and seven of that I had to give to Mum.

"Well, I saved up and had a coat made for my mother in Scotch herringbone tweed by the brother-in-law of one of my friends at work, who was a ladies' tailor. If you could 'ave seen my Mum's face. It was the first new things she'd had. I was then 17 or 18. I'd saved all that time for it.

"One Saturday, soon after I'd given it to her, Mum wanted to go shopping. 'I want you to come with me,' she said. She puts this coat on and gets up to the Blackhorse Road, to the market, and she said 'This is what my Ethel bought me. Brand new it is!'

"Do you know? She went to a stall and she picked out a fawn-coloured hat with a bunch of cherries on it. Cost her 'alf a crown. When she died in the bungalow next door to here, the coat was still in the cupboard — she had worn it and worn it and, each time she put it

50

on, she'd say in a posh voice 'My daughter had this made for me.' She was so proud.

"I thought the world of my mother and would give her anything. I looked after her until she died in 1955. I had a job that somebody else wouldn't have liked: washing your mother after she'd died of dropsy. Just two days before she dies, I was washing her, when she said 'There's no one in this world, who's got such a wonderful daughter as I have.' I replied 'And I've got the most wonderful mother in the world.' I still always put flowers around her photograph in my front room. She died the year after my sister died from cancer. I think it was the shock of that which killed her in the end."

CHAPTER
EIGHT

Lucky Dreams
and Boyfriends

"I used to love dancing and, when I was 14, would go down to the church hall — us three girls used to go, Cousin Flo, Florrie and me, with the kids over the road — to the Threepenny Hop. The boy opposite, Roy, I think, used to play the trumpet or something there. We used to go and encourage him.

"I had an accordion you know. My Dad bought my sister one and my Mum had a row with him about it, 'cos he hadn't bought me one, so he went and got me one. He paid about £3 for it. I was about 16 or 17, I suppose. There was a special book inside that you could teach yourself from. I taught meself, 'cos I had played the piano. I played the accordion a lot until the Second World War, when I put it away. You couldn't play during the war, 'cos you were always in the dugout or at work. When I sold it in the 1990s, the keys were as white as when I first had it. I hadn't played it for years — one of the reasons was that our dog, Bill, didn't like it and used to howl.

52

"I had piano lessons when I was a kid — my Mum paid sixpence a fortnight. Miss Peachley was my teacher. She used to rap my knuckles with a stick if I played the wrong note, wallop! I've still got a lot of the music that I used to play. I was eight years of age when I started. I had a few lessons and didn't like it at first, so I gave up, but went back again later. She was a lovely teacher. I was getting on ever so well — I'd been learning for four years — when I smashed my finger at the toy maker's and couldn't play any more. My sister could play by ear, but I couldn't. We had an old piano that had been given to us, but, with my bad finger, I couldn't practise.

"When I was very young, we never had any radio or television. The first radio we ever had was a crystal set when I was about 12 or 13. My future brother-in-law made it. You used to have to fumble around with a cat's whisker (*a fine adjustable wire in a crystal radio receiver*) to get any sound at all. You had to push the little lever in and move it about until you found a good spot on the crystal. Florrie and I used to go over to Clapton, where Alf lived then, while he was making them. We would sit up in his room and he would give me one earphone and my sister another one and say 'Don't bend the cat's whisker!' If you bent it, you lost all your sound.

"We had no idea that Florrie and Alf were courting for about three years. She didn't tell us, 'cos her chap was her second cousin. Mum didn't agree with it, but Dad did. They married when Florrie was 19. They had two black Daimlers for their wedding — £1.50 it cost them.

"The first proper radio set we had, had a speaker made by wooden leaves pushed into metal ribs. Stuck together, it made a horn. They used to run off the wood in pieces down at the woodyard next to Ensign. You could buy a little tiny set and fit it with the speaker, but it had to be properly done.

"When I first worked at Houghton-Butchers, they used to put me on a bench, where I used to have to stick the wooden leaves into the metal rib of the horn. I used to have to glue all the leaves in. They were similar to the horns on the old-fashioned gramophones, only smaller. I was only doing that for a little while until they got rid of that trade, then I went downstairs onto the presses.

"I never forget, it was during the time that I was making those horns that I was taking Grandad his dinner — he used to live near us then — when I got hit in the eye with a big spinning top that the kids were playing with in the road. They were 'sending messages' they called it — they used to pull this cord and throw the top and I happened to be in the firing line. The next day, I had a black eye and, when I went to work, the manager came up and said 'What have you done to your eye — yer 'usband hit yer?' I said 'I'm not married yet!' Everyone laughed. I was only 14!

"I can see it as if it were only yesterday — Mum catching Florrie and Cousin Flo smoking Lucky Dreams in our front-room when they were teenagers. I remember the packet — it was a lovely blue packet, bluey-mauve with a woman dancing in Indian dress. Mum said 'You can put those out or get out!!' Mum was very strict about that sort of thing.

"Dad was very strict about boys. If I went out in the evening, I had to be back by 10. If I was even the tiniest bit late, I would be in for a tongue-lashing and be docked the amount of time I was late for the next time I went out. When I went out with a boyfriend, I still had to be home by the allocated time and my Dad used to see the shadow of us coming up the garden path and he would be at the front door almost before we got there. There was never any chance of 'hanky panky'!

"I once wore a dress with a two-inch split up from the hem. As soon as Dad saw me wearing it one evening, he made me sew it up before he would permit me to go out. He would not allow petticoats to be seen below hems.

"We never thought of having pre-marital sex, for, if you were not a virgin on your wedding day, you were classed as the lowest of the low.

"I remember there was a young girl once. Her father always used to get blind drunk at The Standard every Saturday night. My Dad used to see him when he walked our elk-hound, Laddie, past Coppermill Lane School. He came home one night and said 'There'll be trouble there,' 'cos the mother used to go and fetch him home and the girl was left to run around the streets. She always had a load of boys around her, even though she was only 12 or 13.

"One morning, my mother met her mother coming along when she was going shopping up the market. I must have been about 17 then — it was after my sister had got married. Mum asked her how she was and she said 'I'm in a hurry — my daughter's been queer and I've left her with a neighbour and must hurry back to see how she is, 'cos she worried me.' My Mum didn't see the woman for some weeks after that and, when she did, the woman said 'You know that day I saw you? When I got home, my neighbour told me to get the doctor. When I asked her why, she told me that she was having a baby.' Yet that girl wasn't yet 14. Her mother said that she never saw no change in her whatsoever. That woman brought the baby up as her own. Years later, the girl had a flat down our road. She had married another man — nobody knew who the father of the baby was and I never knew what happened to it.

"I wasn't like that at all. In fact, Dad told us that if we ever got into trouble, we'd be out! I remember at work in the factory one day, a male colleague walked past me and slapped my bottom. I objected, as that was not allowed, and reported him to my foreman, who thoroughly reprimanded the man. Even though the other girls did not like anything like that happening, I was the only one who ever reported an incident of that kind and for that I was labelled 'The Prude.'

"I was 15 when I started going out with this chap called Bobby. I met him at Ensign. He worked in a different department. I got engaged to him when I was 18 or 19, something like that. If we went to the pictures, he would pay to get in and I would buy the sweets. I used to sit indoors waiting for him to turn up. My friend, Doris, used to say 'He's pulling your leg,' but I wanted evidence that he was cheating on me. I was with him for seven years in all.

"One year, we had to make some royal blue box cameras for Black Cat cigarettes. They were giving them away if you saved so many coupons in packets of cigarettes. To get this big quota out, we had to work all over Easter, then we could have bank holiday Monday off. So I thought 'That's good,' 'cos I was saving up to get married.

"Anyway, when I told this chap that I would be working, he said 'We'll go out on Monday then. I'll be down for you at 2 o'clock and we'll go to the fair at Lea Bridge Road, Leyton.' (My Mum and Dad had gone down to my sister's for the weekend.) By 6 o'clock, he still hadn't turned up. When he did eventually come round, I asked him where he had been. 'Oh,' he said, 'I popped round to my uncle's and couldn't get away.' I noticed that he had dust all over his boots, so I asked 'How did you get your boots so dirty?' He said 'That was when I walked round to my uncle's. I took a short cut.' So I left it at that.

"We never went to the fair — we just went for a walk. On Tuesday, when I went back to work, I spoke to a friend of mine, Lily, who seemed pretty reasonable, and asked her how she enjoyed her bank holiday. She replied 'My friend and I went out and we went to the fair. And we met two fellas. We didn't leave there 'til gone five. We stung 'em proper for money. And, do you know the field opposite?' (There was this field opposite, you could walk through there and that used to bring you to the top of my road in Coppermill Lane, near the reservoir). 'Well,' she said, 'My friend was waiting for the bus and the chap that was with me, walked me across the field and started taking liberties, so I hit him on the chin and knocked him out!' (Lily was a Cockney, you know.) 'Rotten devil — wanted to make us pay for the money he'd spent on us, I suppose.' And then she asked "What did you do on your bank holiday Ethel?"

"While I was telling her what had happened, I showed her a photo with Bobby in it. She said 'That chap in the back row. Is he a friend of yours?' 'Yes,' I replied. 'Well, fancy picking someone like that,' she said. 'How do you mean?' I said. 'Well, you know that fella over the field? That was 'im!' When I told her that he was my fiancé, she said 'Oh, I'm sorry, perhaps I made a mistake.' But I said 'No, you haven't made a mistake, I have,' and I packed him up straight away after that. I had my proof.

"When Dad asked me why I had finished with Bobby, I said 'I have my reasons. I'm not a child.' Dad liked Bobby, and I'm sure that Bobby had told him a different story as to why we had broken up, saying that it was me who had been out with another fella, when in fact I had been out with a girlfriend one evening.

"Dad wasn't happy and accused *me* of cheating. We had an almighty row and I told him — and it was the first time I had ever answered my father back — 'Don't accuse others of what you did yourself!' (I think he thought that I'd forgotten about his affair during the First World War). He went quiet and then I said 'The way you're speaking, it's as if I wasn't your daughter.'

And you know what he said? 'Perhaps you're not,' and my mother sat in the armchair and sobbed her heart out. I'll never forget that as long as I live.

"I put my hand out to slap my father's face, but stopped saying 'No, I can't 'cos you're my father.' I turned to my mother and said 'Look, I'm earning enough money to keep meself. I'll get a place and you can come and live with me.' But she said 'I won't leave my husband.'

"I didn't go out with anybody for about six months after that and then I met Joe, whom I was later to marry. He had got a job in the woodyard that was attached to Ensign and he used to ride a motor bike. He used to stack the wet planks of wood in special drying sheds or kilns as they were delivered, and made desks and dressing tables and all that. Before that, he worked as a builder making shop-fronts for the Co-op.

"Well, I'd been out with Joe on his motor bike and he had just brought me home. As I got me leg over the bike to get off, I felt someone's hands around me throat. It was Bobby. I didn't know what to do, so I stuck me two elbows in his ribs and pushed 'im off. He staggered a bit. Joe was facing the other way and by the time he realised what had happened, Bobby had run off. He was a runner with the Essex Beagles and boy, could he run. Joe said that we'd race after him on the motor bike, but I was so shaken, I just wanted to go home.

"Dad was having his Sunday afternoon nap, when Joe rang the doorbell and said 'Look after your daughter, something's wrong!' He went after him on the bike, but Bobby must have caught the bus at the top of the road.

"We reported the incident to the police and they warned Bobby never to interfere with me again. The copper was at the factory gates every day for a fortnight, but there was no more trouble. However, Bobby's father was a boxer, and I did hear that he gave him a right telling off. After that incident, I had terrible pains in my stomach and was under the doctor for three years."

CHAPTER
NINE

Strikes, Frosts and a Total Eclipse

In May 1926 a General Strike was called and more than two million unionists stopped work in support of the miners. Ethel's father, who was working for Lipton's, came out in sympathy even though he did not belong to a union.

The strike lasted a mere ten days, but its effect on Edwin and his family was felt for much longer. For six months, their only income was that earned by his daughters.

"Mum added a bit extra by making and selling her paper flowers, like the ones she made for Florrie and I at the Peace Tea at the end of World War I. I've still got the button hook she used. She would cut the leaves of the chrysanthemums, put the button hook at the end and pull it down the leaf to make it crinkle.

"For our Christmas dinner in 1926, the man next door, who was employed by the gas works, gave us half of his beef joint, as he was better off than us. With her paper flower money, Mum was able to buy the fruit for our Christmas pudding. I remember taking all the stones out of the sultanas — it made my fingers really sore!

"The following year, Dad started up his own decorating business — 'E. Turner — The People's Decorator' — and then he joined his brother-in-law, Fred, as a decorator in his firm, Nicholls and Sons. All their work was done at Hatch End, Pinner, where a lot of the film stars and opera singers used to live. After two years, Lipton's offered Dad his old job back.

"Dad used to go out early at 6 o'clock in the morning. During the winter of 1926, we had what was called the silver frost. Dad knocked on our bedroom door and he said 'Get up you girls! You've got to slide to work this morning.' He told us to put old socks on our shoes to enable our feet to grip better on the pavements. He said 'Keep going at a trot and you won't fall over.' We did this and we was very lucky not to fall over, 'cos Florrie and I also had to carry our dinners with us. We generally used to take our dinner down to our canteen at work and heat it up. I had sausage and mash in a basin under me arm and my sister had a flask as we would have a cuppa in the morning (we were never allowed to stop work for cups of tea though, just to go to the toilet). I got a fit of the giggles at work afterwards just thinking about it!

"The silver frost was unbelievable — the sight outside. Everything was absolutely white — telegraph poles, everything was shining with silver. I'd never seen anything like it.

"Alice, one of the twins who lived in the flat upstairs, worked at Waterlows in London, where they used to make the banknotes. Alice and Dad caught the same train from St. James Street, Walthamstow, to Old Street, London, where Dad would pick up his van. They would walk up the road together.

"The houses at the top of the road had five stone steps and, as they walked by, a woman opened her front door and came down the steps to the gate to fetch the milk (that's when we used to have three milk deliveries a day, if we wanted it!) As she did so, she slipped on the icy steps and her nightdress went up over her head. Alice covered her eyes when Dad said 'Don't look Alice!' He went and helped the woman up and pulled her nightdress back down again. I can always remember him telling us that. It was funny, that was!

"I also remember my mother placing some small sheets of glass over tiles in the kitchen and smoking the glass by holding a candle over them. This was to protect our eyes whilst watching the total eclipse in 1927."

CHAPTER
TEN

Friends, Fun and Frolics

When Ethel was about 17, she had an encounter with a pet black-bird, which her paternal grandfather once found on his allotment: "My grandfather used to go down to the allotment and pick young fresh dandelion leaves to use as lettuce. He never bought lettuce. 'Dandelion leaves are much better than lettuce,' he said. He hardly ever ate fried eggs either. When he used to fry a bit of bacon, he used apple rings instead of eggs to go with it. That was his breakfast on Sunday mornings.

"Anyway, one morning, he discovered a young blackbird on the allotment. It had obviously been abandoned, so he took it home with him and looked after it until it got bigger. As he didn't like keeping it in a cage in his flat, he gave it to my Dad. The bird wouldn't have lived in the wild again, 'cos it was so tame. My Dad hung the cage outside by the brick wall of the outside toilet in the summer and used to take it inside in the winter. One autumn, I'd gathered a lot of blackberries to make some wine with. I'd strained them and was going to strain them again that night. I was wearing a nice cream linen dress for work and the wine was on the table covered with a bit of muslin. The blackbird's cage had been brought into the kitchen, because it was getting cold, and Dad had given the bird a snail to eat, which it did using the stone in its cage to crack open the shell.

"While I was seeing to the wine, Mum warned me to watch out for flying bits of snail shell. As I got up on a stool to look inside the cage, it came off its hook into my arms and I fell backwards tipping the bowl of blackberry wine all over me head and me lovely linen dress! Luckily Mum managed to get all the stain out by soaking the dress in salt water in her old copper!"

Another amusing incident occurred one night, when, as a young woman in the 1920s, Ethel had been "out on the razzle" with some friends: "I remember ever so clearly — I'd been out and got in at 10 o'clock, 'cos you went to bed early then, when you'd been working hard, and this night, Mum and Dad had gone to bed.

"Dad never used to turn his light out, he used to sit there with his watch — 'See the time, you're a minute late,' he used to say. Anyway, I went into the bedroom and switched my light on . . . we had those casement windows, you know, and mine was open a little bit to let in the fresh air (it was summer time, see). Well, what happened was, I pulled the bedclothes back to get in and there was this spider. I've never seen one so big in all my life and I'm not exaggerating. Its legs were *huge* and they was all *hairy*! I screamed and pushed the bedclothes back. Now I don't dislike spiders and I

65

really don't like to kill 'em, but I couldn't touch that one, it was *massive*; it must have been a foreign one come over in a box of bananas delivered to the grocer's at the top of Edward Road. I flew into Mum and Dad's room calling 'Dad! Dad! Quick!!'

"Now, my Dad used to wear those old-fashioned shirts with the collar attached (I used to 'ave to scrub 'em) and they always had long back tails. He always went to bed in 'is shirt and my parents' bed was one of those on the old-fashioned wooden frames with the springs. My Mum was rather on the plump side and used to sleep against the wall. Me Dad jumped out of bed so quick and me poor ol' Mum was tipped into the corner!

"Suddenly realising that he'd only got his shirt on, me Dad pulled the tail of it between his legs to hide his privates — and I've never forgotten the way he ran down the hallway, it was so funny! My Mum had a good sense of humour and I can laugh too. It's a good job I can, what with some of the things I've been through!

"Anyway, when Dad came out of my room, he said that he'd knocked the spider to the floor with his slipper and crushed it. Honest to God, it had black hairs on its legs and was *that* size. It certainly frightened the life out of me and my Dad, and we don't scare easy!"

Ethel's great sense of humour and fun was also to be put to good use raising money for charity, in particular, for the Connaught Hospital, of which she became a Life Governor in 1939. With her late friend Doris,

Ethel used to parade in Walthamstow Carnival each year: "The first year Doris dressed up as a soldier and I went as an English lady in a petticoat (I showed me knickers!). I also wore a crinoline bonnet and carried a parasol. I must have been 19 or 20 then. The following year, I was a Spanish man complete with black hat, jacket and mandolin and for the final time, Doris and I entered as the Bisto Kids. We sent away for the clothes for that, but we had to find our own shoes. They sent us the wigs and everything. I made a sawdust pie with pastry on top and stuck wire in it with cotton wool on top to look like smoke. And we won second prize! Doris's nephew had a little barrow. Doris asked if we could borrow it to push me up to the podium to collect our prizes. It was so small, I couldn't get out of it afterwards, 'cos me hips stuck!! The other funny thing was, we won a camera from Ensign, where I had worked since I was 14!"

Ethel and Doris got up to many more pranks with their friends and colleagues when they went on their many days out together before the start of the Second World War: "When us girls had our Sundays out, we used to go sometimes to the Kursaal at Southend. If there happened to be a ride that hadn't attracted many people, Doris used to ask the attendant to let us girls go on for half fare in return for shoutin' and hollerin' a bit to attract more trade. We used to go on those rides where your skirts blew up, like on the Big Wheel. We thought it was real funny. We never used to wear trousers in those days, we had dresses on!

67

"But they wouldn't let us go on the railway thing — roller coaster, I think you'd call it now — 'cos it was too expensive. Very high it was. My chap Joe, took me on it once, 'cos I said I hadn't been on it before, but he didn't want to sit in the front. When our turn came, he had to sit in the front seat 'cos it was the only one left. Joe was terrified and turned really green. When he got off, he couldn't stand. The ride was terrific and I really enjoyed it, but I wouldn't go on it now!

"We never 'ad much money, so we couldn't go on a lot. Once, as we went out of the Kursaal, Doris and I got on the weighing machine together and broke it, so we ran out!

"We used to travel by train on our days out. We'd pick the tram up at the top of the turning, where the market was in Walthamstow, and travelled to Stratford to board the train. That was when we were going to Walton-on-the-Naze. But when we went to Southend, I used to walk to the Blackhorse Road to catch the train. London, Midland and Scottish (LMS) was the name of the railway company, and it took you right into Southend.

"Anyway, when we travelled to Walton, I crocheted hats for all of us and sewed a white feather on the top. Then, when we were riding on the top of the tram to Stratford, we would be able to see the members of our crowd. I used to say 'There's another one — she's got a white feather in her hat!' If we lost someone coming home, I'd know because there'd be a white feather missing when I'd counted them all. There were usually 24 of us, you see. And do you know — I remember every one. One used to do the bookwork for the convent school for the poor kids. She was a good person, she was.

"Coming back once from a trip to the seaside, Doris was saying how hungry she felt. We got in a carriage that had a little side toilet to it. As there was no light in the main carriage, we put the light on in the cubicle and left the door open. Our manager's secretary — I'll never forget her, she was so la-di-da — wanted to come with us. None of us liked her very much, especially Doris, 'cos she was so stuck up. Well, as Doris was hungry, she decided to eat this hard-boiled egg she had with her, but just as she was about to put it into her mouth, this girl yawned. Doris saw her opportunity and, in the dim light of the carriage, threw the egg at her. 'How disgusting!' the girl said. That started us all off and we had this amazing food fight with everything we had in our bags! Then, just before we got to Stratford, we cleared up the carriage — the windows, everything. We never did no damage, we just used to have some good fun, you know!

"In the winter, when we couldn't go to the seaside, we used to go up to London, to the theatre. My friend, Joan, who was the manager of a nice shop in London (I've still got a nice pair of scissors from there) said that if ever we wanted to go to the theatre, we were to inform her and she would book us our tickets for sixpence . . . We used to go to work on a Friday and our foreman used to say 'Where you goin' tonight girls?' After work, we'd walk up Wood Street, near Forest Road, all of us together, and catch the train to go to the theatre. We'd make sure that our seats were booked, then go to the large Lyons Corner House to have something to eat like fish 'n' chips.

"We saw some lovely shows. I remember there being one show with nude people in it, but we wouldn't go to that one! We did see Dulcie Gray and her husband (Michael Denison) once and we did go to the White Horse theatre a couple of times too. As there were a lot of us, we got in a bit cheaper. We was artful then, but we didn't 'ave much pocket money, see. I didn't earn my full wages of 28 shillings a week 'til I was 21. I started on eight shillings a week and, until I came of age, I received tuppence an hour more each birthday. I worked from eight o'clock until half past five, Saturdays 'til half past 12, and you weren't allowed to leave until you'd made sure that your desk was all clean and tidy ready for Monday.

"We was goin' up to Wood Street to catch the train once, when Doris bought some stink bombs and jumping crackers from a shop near the station. She said that when we went through the tunnel at Hackney Downs Station, we'd let these crackers off in the train. She told me to sit on one side of the door and she would sit on the other. When it all went dark in the tunnel, we let the crackers off. The girls screeched and, when the train had passed through and it was light again, I saw that one girl was hanging onto the luggage rack! A jumping cracker had burnt a hole in her coat. Were we sorry, but we still chucked the two stink bombs into the carriage just as we got out at Liverpool

Street! I tell you, that snobby girl never came with us again!

"Doris was the one who suggested all those pranks, not me. And there was another one called May — she was just as mad. May was a lovely person, a real tomboy. She was six feet tall and full of life and fun. Whenever you went out with May and Doris, you knew you were going to have a good time. I used to do all the organising and they used to arrange all the fun.

"When we went to Walton-on-the-Naze one summer, there were some photographers from the Walton Gazette up on the cliffs, who asked if they could take some photographs of us. Doris arranged us all for the pictures. Lots of other people wanted to take our photos too, as they could see what a fun time we were having! We would take any unused film from the cameras that were brought into Ensign for repair out in the darkrooms and use it up on our days out.

"Doris, May and I played for the Ensign Netball Team — I became the captain eventually. Doris played Goal Shooter. May only played for a little while. We used to play behind The Billet (*public house*). Doris and I thoroughly enjoyed that, but when Doris suddenly took a fancy to walking, we both dropped out of netball. The team weren't all that good, so it was quite easy to give it up.

"Doris was marvellous at walking. I wasn't all that sporty really. Doris was the sporty one and so was May. Doris rode a Matchless motor bike when she was 14 (she was four years older than me). The motor bike had a long red tank. She used to rev up and down our road like mad and make me roll up.

"Doris was a good runner too. She won quite a few races on sports day. She always used to go nice and brown in the summer — you could always pick her out in photos. I was no good at running or walking. Cousin Flo was the runner in our family. I went to keep fit classes mostly. I was about 15 or 16 when I went to the school at Mission Grove to do keep fit. Doris would come along sometimes — when she wasn't out walking!

"If I went out with Doris to go to a dance, she would take the man's part and I would take the lady's. I used say to her 'You know that I'm not allowed out after 10 o'clock?' Sometimes, a friend of Doris's, who was a Freemason, would give her two free tickets for the dances at the Masonic Hall. The chap I was engaged to only came round once a week, so I used to go with Doris. We were back late once or twice and she came home with me. One night after a dance at the Chequers Pub in the market, we arrived back late. We'd got some balloons and Doris shut one in the door — I thought it was going to wake up Dad, but we were lucky that time!

"Trouble was, some of the dances used to be on a Wednesday night and we'd got to go to work in the morning. Dad used to get up early to go to work and, as he walked past our bedroom door, he would bang on it. 'Get up you girls! You'll be late!' He used to make out that he was going out by slamming the front door and then he would creep back in. He made sure you got up, my Dad did. He was good in that way. My

72

foreman used to say 'You've never been late once in all the 18 years you've been here.' Yet Doris was always late when she lived with her sister.

"Doris died aged 94. She was in a nursing home. The last time I saw her, she still had the same mischievous laugh. May died many years ago. She left me some money and I bought an exercise machine with it!"

CHAPTER
ELEVEN

More Cameras, Pineapples and Nice Hot Rolls

"I used to love to go to work, but we had to be through the gates before eight o'clock in the morning or pay a fine a threepence.

"Being a tester, I had to make sure that the cameras were all perfect, that no light could get in and that they were all clean and polished. There were all different types of cameras — big ones, little tiny ones, box cameras. We used to go into the darkrooms to test them.

"One day, I went up to Wood Street at lunchtime and brought back a pineapple. I started to cut it up in the darkroom with a small pocket knife I had. Just as we were about to eat it, the foreman came in. 'This is what you do when you're supposed to be working!' he said. Then he rolled up and said 'I don't mind as long as you give me a lump!'

"Every Saturday morning before eight o'clock after I'd got out at the station at Wood Street, I used to pop into the baker's on the corner and buy half a dozen rolls. Then I'd go into the dairy next door and buy half a pound of butter. I'd get to work, take all my purchases into the darkroom five minutes before we were due to start, and cut and butter the nice hot rolls for our breakfast. The foreman used to say 'I don't know why you're hiding in there, 'cos I know what you're doing and I'd like one of those rolls!' His name was George and he always had his breakfast of a hot roll with us every Saturday morning!

"I was very fond of whistling while I was doing the cameras and once, when I had just started work, I was whistling away cleaning the cameras and George was upstairs in the focussing department. The darkrooms were under the stairs and, when he had got so many cameras finished, he would have to come downstairs to test them for light in the darkrooms, see. Well, this particular time when he came downstairs, he heard me whistling and said sternly 'You're not paid to sit there whistling, get on with your work!!' I told my colleagues 'I don't like that foreman one bit,' but in the end we got on ever so well with him, when I realised that he was really nice and didn't mind what you did as long as you got the job done.

"Sometimes they'd take you off what you were doing and put you in another department, to make sure that you could do all the jobs and not just one. Once, I was put on packing — the times I cut my fingers on the paper!

"But I really loved my job at Ensign, working with all the girls and everything. We never 'ad no rows, not one and no one took advantage of you. However, when our manager left, we had a new one, who was a right so and so. He gave me a camera and said 'Do that now!' I said that I wouldn't do it while he was watching me. He was one of those people who look at you as if you are a bit of dirt. He never used to say thank you.

"The second time he demanded that I check this important camera for the Gold Coast immediately, I told him 'I'll bring it up to you when I've finished it and I'll not do it with you standing behind me!' When I took it up to him, I demanded a pay rise, and I got it!"

CHAPTER
TWELVE

Motor Bikes
and Primus Stoves

Joe Elvin had been working in the woodyard next to Ensign, when he met Ethel. When the woodyard had to make him redundant, because of the decreasing supply of wood, Ethel managed to get him a job at Ensign:

"Joe had always loved doing small work and, as a hobby, used to make radios, so I thought that he might like a job working with cameras.

"Joe was an inspector of the air force cameras — he used to make and repair them during the Second World War. Oh — he loved all that. Great big things they were.

"He always had every Sunday off and he belonged to this crowd — his brother and sister-in-law, his nephew, Charlie and Edna — there was a big crowd of them and they all used to go out together on Sunday in the summer to seaside places like Walton and Frinton. Some had motor bikes and some had motor bikes with sidecars. They would all take their own food and park in the car parks there, spread their picnic out on cloths and have a bit of everybody's. Proper merry crowd they were.

"Well, on the days that Doris's chap used to work, Doris would ride on the back of Joe's bike. One day, we'd been working on Saturday morning up until 12 o'clock, when Doris said 'There's that chap waiting who I go out with on Sundays.' She told him 'No, I can't come tomorrow; Stan's not working this week. Take Ethel instead.' Joe said that he would take anybody who wanted to come. 'I'll make sure that she comes,' Doris said. Joe told me that he'd be waiting for me at Forest Road at eight o'clock in the morning. So I said 'Well, don't wait too long — I probably won't be there.' I didn't know what to wear or what I was going to take, but Mum said 'Go on, you go! But I shall worry 'til you get back, 'cos you'll be on a motor bike.'

"I did go. We went to Walton-on-the-Naze. Mum said 'Give him some cigarettes or something. That'll pay for your day out. We won't tell your father,' 'cos my Dad wouldn't have 'ad it, see. Well, I got on this bloomin' motor bike and told Joe 'Don't go too fast!' He said 'If you're frightened, put your arms around me waist and stick your fingers in me belt!' I remember hanging on like mad. We never had any helmets or anything — just leather coats and berets. Once I ripped the sole off my new sandals goin' round a corner! But they weren't fast drivers and it was all country lanes then. We picked up the gang at the Green Gate, Ilford. I said to Joe 'When we come back, don't you dare drop me near my home — my Dad'll kill me if he sees me on a motor bike!' So he dropped me off at the top of the road and said

'Come again if you feel like it.' I said 'All right, but I mustn't let my Dad know.' Mum was a good coverer though. We used to get back about six or seven in the evening, 'cos we all had to go to work the next day.

"I used to really enjoy those outings. They were such a lovely crowd. I've still got the Primus stove we took to boil up the water for our tea. On the way home, we used to sing — Joe's favourite song was 'The Very Thought of You' by Bing Crosby."

Ethel and Joe became engaged some three years later. The single diamond engagement ring came from Walkers, the Hoe Street jewellers. Their betrothal lasted for two years before they married during the Second World War in September 1940 at St. Michael's Church, Walthamstow, where the weddings of Ethel's parents and her sister Florrie had taken place.

Part Three

1939–1945

CHAPTER
THIRTEEN

Doodlebugs
and Dugouts

"When you got home from work, before you'd even had time to change, it would be 'Oh, blow — there it goes again (the air raid siren).' So you'd quickly put on your dugout clothes and go into the shelter. You couldn't even make yourself a cup of tea and you weren't allowed to listen to the wireless in the dugouts. They used to switch off the stations then, in case the Germans picked it up.

"It was frightening, especially when you had those buzz-bombs or doodlebugs. You could hear them coming, and when you heard them shut off, you thought 'Oh God, is this our one?' And you'd wait for it to go bang, but you would always think 'It might be us next'. And that's how it went on. In the end, you did become a little hardened to it and you might say 'Let's go to bed and take a chance!' But we never actually did take that chance — just in case.

"We came out of the dugout at about six in the morning. Mostly, we just talked and dozed. Directly we used to nod off, a bomb would drop and wake you up.

In the winter-time, the raids started at about six when it was dark."

The Anderson Shelter or dugout as it was known was made of corrugated steel and stood in a pit four feet deep. As it didn't have a proper floor, only earth, it flooded whenever it rained. During the London Blitz in 1940, the city was bombed every night for more than two months.

"Eight of us used to sit in the shelter, very often with our feet in water. It was so very crowded and we could hardly move sat on these wooden benches. As for going to the loo — you had to wait until there was a lull in the bombing and then dash outside! If we had time, we would make up drinks to take into the dugout with us — we used to use any old mugs. There was no heating at all, so we would put old thick socks on our feet to keep warm, but then they would get wet, so we'd have to take them off! Of course, as there were so many of us in there, we generated our own heat, which would then cause condensation to drip on our heads!

"At The Elms cricket ground at the back of where I lived, there were playing fields and the River Lea beyond, where there were horse-drawn barges. The Germans dropped a load of bombs there, 'cos they thought it was the Thames — it stretched almost to Edmonton. So when we were in the dugout during a heavy raid, we were being shaken about through the impact of the bombs exploding. Your head resounded with the 'Bang! Bang!' as you sat there with your feet in water. After the war was over, I think that about four to five hundred unexploded bombs were found there.

"There were Molotov baskets (Incendiary Bombs) and they used to come down all alight and you could only put sand on them to put them out. Land mines, rockets, buzz-bombs — we had the lot!

"I was sitting in front of the cooker crocheting once when the air raid warning sounded. Mum said 'I'm not going in the dugout tonight — I'm fed up sitting with me feet in water.' All of a sudden, we heard an explosion, flew up the passageway and got down on our knees. Mum was in front and me behind, we were almost lying down. We could hear another one coming and as we listened, I looked at my hand — my crochet hook was just inches away from my Mum's bottom! I'll never forget that as long as I live.

"We sat in the dugout and Dad would say he was going for a walk to make sure everyone was all right. If people were frightened and a bit nervous, he'd go and talk to them and all that sort of thing, you know. He was very good and got a medal for it, 'cos I found it in one of his drawers when he died."

Joe, for his part, joined the National Fire Service (NFS) after failing his medical for the services because of a leg injury. He completed his training at Forest Road Fire Station in Walthamstow and was the leading fireman at Ensign, where he made, repaired and inspected air force cameras: "He fell down the iron staircase, where he worked and twisted his leg two weeks before his number was called up for the Air Force. They made you stand on one leg and swing the other and he couldn't stand on his bad leg, so they asked him to come back in three months time. During those three months, they dropped his age group (he was six years older than me) so he had a choice of going in the Fire Service or the Home Guard. Where he worked at Ensign, they wanted him in the fire service, so he chose that which meant that he could do a bit of work as well as be a fireman.

"Joe loved his fire service. I remember later, when we came to Doddinghurst and the chimney caught alight, he knew just what to do — he took out all the front and stuck wet sacks up it. It was when I had an Aga and it was Christmas morning and I was cooking me chicken in it and it made the chimney breast red hot upstairs. And he knew what to do — he was really clever.

"He never really said anything about his fire service work, except when a bomb dropped on Ensign on the place where they kept all the liquids, spirits and that for the work. It all caught alight and he got his shoes burnt ... his feet got red hot, but as he was leading fireman, he had to stand there you see. He used to tow this big tender with a truck. Directly the siren went he was on duty. We used to come down to Doddinghurst sometimes for a sleep in the shed to get away from all the noise, though we weren't supposed to. You weren't supposed to come out of your area if you were a fireman, but we didn't do it often.

"Because the work I was doing at Ensign was classed as luxury trade, they closed down our floor, which is why I went into ammunitions. I was the last one to go.

I also worked as an inspector in a munitions factory in Billet Road, Walthamstow, where I oversaw the making of tracer bullets and gun parts. I used to do a fortnight of days and a fortnight of nights. I was there when I got married. I was there for about a fortnight and they put me on as inspector. I used to set all the machines up in the morning or at night. I loved it. I would inspect all the little parts that went in the bombs and we assembled them. I used to have to check them all and check the girls to make sure they did their work.

"I was paid by the Woolwich Arsenal by cheque once a month through the Post Office. They got me the job at the Labour Exchange. I had to have an examination by a doctor before I went there and I had to make a will to say what I was going to leave to my Mum. In the middle of a raid, we used to have to rush out and go into the dugout, where I would sit crocheting.

"When I was on nights, I would work from eight at night 'til eight in the morning. When I was on days, it would be from eight in the morning 'til eight at night for another fortnight. And I also made ammunition boxes for Cabinet Industries Ltd on the Arterial Road, with Cousin Flo."

CHAPTER
FOURTEEN

Roses and Wedding Cakes

"I didn't leave Mum 'til I was 30, 'cos I loved her so much. I had my wedding dress made by old friends of ours, who were court dressmakers up in London, and my sister's bridesmaid's outfit — her dress, headdress, her gloves, shoes, everything — she was my matron of honour. I was going to have a little one to hold my train. She was three, but her mother had to go away, because they evacuated mothers who were expecting babies.

"I bought all the flowers, even the buttonholes, as well as the wedding breakfast. It was with the money I'd saved since I was a toddler. The only thing I borrowed, was my sister's wedding veil. We went and saw a bedroom suite we wanted in Hoe Street and we hadn't got quite enough money — we wanted another £3, I think it was. So my Dad said 'I'll loan you the £3, but I want it back,' so I went and paid for it and got it delivered to out flat, and I paid my father back with my first week's wages afterwards.

"My father grew us some flowers on his allotment and we had those on the tables. The flowers in my bouquet came from Alda's florist in Hoe Street. I remember my bouquet cost £2 and 10 shillings and my sister's was £1 and 10 shillings. My bouquet consisted of red roses and white heather and Florrie wore a dress of lavender and her bouquet was all lovely tea roses.

"When we were standing at the altar, the warning went and the bombs were dropping. We couldn't have the church bells and we couldn't have the choir, because they had all been evacuated, so all we had was the organ.

"Oh, and I'll never forget it. I'll tell you what happened. It was a High Church, St. Michael's and All Angels mind, and they burnt incense in there. There was a man who waited at the door to lead you in. He was a little man in a little hat with a knob on the top. I was holding my Dad's arm and we were walking up the aisle and this little man tripped and I had a fit of the giggles and couldn't stop laughing. Because I couldn't have little Jean holding my train, I'd sown a tape onto my train and held it on my little finger. When I got to the church, I let it go down. As we got to the altar — you have to walk up two or three steps to get to the altar — I remembered seeing in a film once at the pictures, one woman standing on some else's train and pulling the back out. I was standing at the altar thinking of that — I don't know why — and I said to my chap 'When you move, don't tread on my train!' And he did just that. I whispered 'Get off! Get off!' When I got home and looked, I had footmarks right in the middle

89

of me train. I never forgot that. There was three, if not four yards, of material in the train."

Later on, brides were unable to buy traditional wedding dresses with trains because the amount of material they required had been rationed.

"I had one of those collars that stood up at the back, stiff, Queen Anne style, and all little buttons along the sleeves, which came down in points over my hands. And, at the bottom, I had a little frill, all the way round. And I had a twisted silver cord around me waist with tassels.

"When my sister got married, my mother waited at the tables. When I got married, I said 'You don't do that. You're equal to us.' My Mum was lovely. She bought a big tin of ham. She cooked sausages and all that and sliced them. We had jelly and blancmange, you know. She bought the stuff and stored it before the wedding. And the lady upstairs waited on the tables. We all sat down. I borrowed the trestles and the stools from the church around the corner and brought them round to our home on a trolley. I managed to buy the last white wedding cake from Hayes, the baker — he was one of the old-fashioned bakers. It was a two-tier one. One of the girls from upstairs, Mary, who got married after me, had to have a chocolate one, 'cos I went to her wedding. (*Many later had to make do with cardboard wedding cakes*). Everybody went home at nine o'clock because of the air raids.

"I got fish knives and forks and my chap got a bedside lamp as wedding presents. The lamp was all crystal pink. I had been due to collect a wedding

90

present from some ex-neighbours of ours. I had visited them some two weeks before and it had been time for me to leave, 'cos I had to catch the tram in order to be home on time.

"Unfortunately, the bus was late — probably due to an air raid — so I ran all the way from my stop home all in the pitch black, because I knew I would be in trouble with Dad for being late. I arrived home with one minute to spare, completely breathless. Dad was sitting in the front room with his watch in hand! I later discovered that the family I had been visiting, had been killed by a bomb, which dropped on their house while they were sheltering in the cellar. The girl was a pretty little thing. I used to push her in her pram when she was little. She had wanted to be a bridesmaid at my wedding.

"We got married on the Saturday and went back to work on the Monday, though we did have a few days honeymoon in Cheddar Gorge a little later — by motor bike, of course."

It was to be one of their last outings for a while, for Joe had to sell his bike because of the petrol rationing. In 1942, people had to prove that driving was essential to either their work or health, in order to obtain petrol coupons.

CHAPTER
FIFTEEN

Boots, Bugs
and Knickers!

"We only spent the first night of our marriage in our rented flat in Courtenay Road — it took me a year to make the mats for it. We had two bombs after that, within days of each other. One was almost a direct hit — it landed in our back garden and took out our back windows; the second landed farther up the road and took out our front windows. So, we had no windows, just boards up. For a while, we lived with Mum and Dad, but spent most of the time, when we weren't working, in their dugout.

"Then on the 20th April 1941, Hitler's birthday, we had the 'land mine' (*even more than a terror weapon than the doodlebugs, the huge naval mine or 'land mine' as it was known, fell slowly and silently by parachute and always came in pairs. The blast from it could blow a man a quarter of a mile. The mine of which Ethel speaks exploded in Cornwallis Road at 3.50am. The gardens of the houses in Courtenay and Cornwallis Roads backed onto one another. Ethel and*

Joe's flat was situated just a couple of houses down from where the mine landed).

"It was very early in the morning and Joe was sick of sitting in the dugout and was just going to go back to bed, when we heard this swinging sort of noise. 'Get back in quick!' I said, 'There's something comin' down!' There was this almighty explosion and I said 'That's our flat gone!' Joe wouldn't believe it. Then, when the all clear sounded, we went to see. All the houses had collapsed. The crater was so big, a bus had fallen into it. Our neighbours' house was flattened and we saw the remains of their bodies in the trees. Her and her husband — he was a taxi driver — you never forget a sight like that. (*According to records, the blast killed four people and injured 24. The twin was never found, but it was thought to have fallen in the reservoir).*

"Returning from Reading one day, I also saw the terrible aftermath of a Hoe Street bomb, which killed a bus-load of people and others queuing outside a fish and chip shop.

"We'd been living with Mum and Dad for a while, and then a friend of mine who I worked with, got us a flat in Woodford. Luckily, most of our furniture had been put into storage after the first two bombs, though we lost all the curtains I'd made. Our flat in Woodford was in a big house made into four flats. The air raids eased up a bit then. We had a sort of gap. But we had to move from there because they had a big water tank over our bedroom and it kept leaking — I used to go into me bedroom with Wellington boots at the side of me bed, 'cos of the water. Once, we got called home from work, 'cos our room was all flooded.

"Then my other friend, Doris, told me about another upstairs flat in Roberts Road, Walthamstow, next to her flat. The funny thing was, the day we moved, as the van drew up, my friend came running out and she said 'Oh, I forgot to tell you — this flat is riddled with bugs!'

The following weekend, my hubby sent me out to my Mum's for the day and he got a blowlamp to burn out the bugs. He went up into the loft and killed them all. Trouble was, he set fire to the loft by catching a window frame alight too! We thought that being a fireman, he knew what he was doing! The damage wasn't too bad, thank goodness, and we lived there for about three or four years 'til the end of the war.

"We had more raids then, 'cos I used to sit on the stairs there with me tin hat on and a tin on me lap with all me papers in, 'cos the lady downstairs wouldn't let me go in the dugout. She had four children, so there was no room for me until they were evacuated. Mum was half an hour away then, so I couldn't use her dugout. So, when Joe went on duty, I would sit on the stairs on me own. I could hear the anti-aircraft guns going by, but although I wanted to see one, I never did in all those years.

"It was also when we were at Roberts Road that I can remember when Cousin Flo and I had just got on the bus along the Arterial Road going towards Edmonton and they dropped a bomb. We knew it was at The Billet somewhere and I was thinking of my chap, wondering if he was all right. I always used to sit underneath the stairs on the bus — I thought it was safer. When they dropped this bomb at The Billet, we were standing on the platform waiting to get off. The bus was swaying all over the road to avoid where the bomb had dropped. Then it stopped and poor Flo fell in a bed of nettles!

"My sister lived out in the country a bit, Stoke Row near Henley-on-Thames, and Cousin Flo lived with her for a while. With all the upset of the war an' all, going to work, trying to do housework, looking after my grandfather and rushing in and out of the dugouts, and all the upset of the bombs, I did get ill. I was being so violently sick in the end that I was bringing up solids. The doctor put me on a special diet of steamed fish and egg custards for six weeks. He told me to get away for a while — 'It will do you good,' he said. I did write to my sister, but because she had also taken in two evacuees as well as Cousin Flo, there was no room. That was just after we were married. My Mum never got ill, she was pretty good — perhaps she was able to cope with it a bit better."

Shortly after Ethel and Joe's wedding, an amusing — if not embarrassing — incident occurred: "I hadn't been married for very long and I had me crêpe de chine pants on — French knickers they were called. I'd bought meself a whole new set of underclothes for me wedding. They was only kept up by two little buttons at the side. I'd worn them to work and had just got off the tram at The Billet and was walking up Blackhorse Road, when I could feel somethin' slippin'. As I was walking up the slope to go down the turning where I lived, me pants fell down — luckily I had some little ones underneath. I kicked them off, rolled 'em up and tucked them under me arm and walked down the other side of the station where nobody was and went home! I was so embarrassed. Ever since then, no matter where I go, I always fasten me pants with a little pin and I've done that for donkeys' years!"

CHAPTER
SIXTEEN

Rissoles, Swedes and Rhubarb Wine

At the start of the war, a national register was established and everyone was issued with an identity card. One of the reasons for this was that the government was worried about spies. The national register number was printed on the front of the ration book along with a serial number and local office number.

"I certainly didn't like the national loaf — it was much too gritty. But it was amazing how far you could stretch a tin of meat. My Dad had an allotment and he grew what he could from seedlings — potatoes and all that. I used to make potato pie and we had mashed potato sandwiches. And sometimes, I would make rissoles from a tiny bit of mince from our rations, an egg, if I was lucky enough to get one, and potatoes. I would mix it all up, make it in pats and roll them in flour and fry them. They were lovely. I tried horsemeat once. I couldn't eat it. I'd rather do without.

"We would sometimes have mashed swede as a change from potato. We used to eat a lot of swedes —

pigs like them, you know. When we kept pigs later on, my chap would buy sacks of them, chop 'em all up and put them in the meal and they used to love 'em. (*During the war, people were encouraged to empty their kitchen scraps into 'pig bins' situated along the streets. Many also joined 'pig clubs', where members bought and then fattened up a pig*).

"You were lucky to get one proper egg a week, but if you went to the doctor with tummy trouble, you got an extra ration of egg. I used to have to line up for bread. And they used to give the children orange juice and cod liver oil, I remember that.

"The dried milk used to be nice. I used to get dried milk and cocoa and make chocolate for my grandfather (paternal). He used to say 'I'll give you my sweet coupons, girl.' He liked my chocolate better than the bought stuff — said that was too sweet. Grandfather was really lovely. He was so appreciative of what you did for him. I used to get all his shopping for him and Mum would get me to drop his meals in and do his cleaning. She would visit on Mondays, Wednesdays and Fridays and I would go on Tuesdays, Thursdays and Saturdays, when I would get his pension — sometimes, I would get him some corned beef. On Sunday, my Mum would do a roast dinner and Dad would take it to him with a pint of beer.

"I would make him an apple tart every week too, and Dad would give me the rhubarb he'd grown on his allotment and I'd make wine with it. I used to make a gallon of rhubarb wine and every week would take Grandfather a pint bottle. He swore that's what made him live 'til 92! Grandfather died just after I got married. Gran died before the war.

"During the war, my grandfather had been shopping in the market in Walthamstow and just as he walked past the Lord Palmerston Pub on the corner, a German fighter plane flew down with its guns firing. Grandfather ran and hid behind the wall of the pub to escape, but, after it had gone, he stood out in the middle of the road and shook his fist at it. Cor, was he mad! He was flaming!!" *Clothes too were rationed from 1941. Everyone was allocated "points" in the form of coupons to purchase whatever they needed and there were posters proclaiming "Make Do and Mend':* "I used to use a black pen to draw a line down the back of my legs, so it looked as if I had stockings on. I thought it was a bit too messy to use brown cream or gravy powder and water."

CHAPTER
SEVENTEEN

Big Bands
and Booby Traps

During the First World War, there had been no radio or television. In the Second World War, the wireless became both a source of information and entertainment. Music provided a distraction from the realities of deprivation and conflict and dance halls vibrated with the sounds of the Big Bands.

"Henry Hall and his Orchestra were my favourite. A girl I used to work with, her brother used to play the saxophone in his band. I also used to like Billy Cotton and Geraldo. I used to like dancing to all the Big Band music. I liked Gracie Fields — I would go and see her films before the war — and I thought that Vera Lynn's 'The White Cliffs Of Dover' was wonderful.

"I used to love listening to all the music on the wireless, but sometimes, when you switched on the radio, you would hear the voice of Lord Haw Haw — 'This is Haw Haw talking, Germany calling'. (*William Joyce, known as Lord Haw Haw, was a Nazi broadcaster. He was born in the USA of Irish parents and became a supporter of the British fascist Sir*

Oswald Mosley. He obtained a British passport and, in 1939, went to Germany and broadcast Nazi propaganda to Britain during the Second World War. After the war, he was tried and executed for treason).

"Haw Haw used to say 'We're going to bomb you tonight' and other such threats. I can still hear his voice even now. I think that he even told us when the buzz-bombing was going to start. It was a bad thing to do, because it put the wind up you. It certainly did me. I was learning typing in the evenings on the top floor of this big college in Forest Road, Walthamstow, at the time, and it put me off going — I thought they were going to drop a bomb on it.

"When you turned the wireless on and you heard Churchill giving his speech, you would look at people's faces as they went to work the next day and they would say 'Did you hear him? Wasn't he marvellous?' Churchill kept us going all those years — he was a wonderful man."

Just as Churchill stirred the patriotic emotions in the British, Hitler became the reason for German hatred: "Cousin Flo could really swear when she wanted to and when a lorry-load of German prisoners-of-war drove by us in Walthamstow one day, she really let rip at them. But then her younger brother, Herbert, had just been killed. Herbert was a motor bike courier. He'd got blown off his motorcycle and had been home on leave. He hadn't long been back, when they heard before the rest of us that the war had ended. Despite warnings, he and three friends got into a booby-trapped motor vehicle

101

and it exploded. Three were killed, including Herbert, and the other one was badly injured. Two days later we heard that the war was over."

CHAPTER
EIGHTEEN

Fancy Dress
and Fireworks

The end of the Second World War was a relief for everyone. VE-Day on May 8th 1945, was a day filled with parties, fireworks and Union Jacks flying everywhere: "I paid in for my two nephews — I think I paid in about five shillings a week for about three months — 'cos I didn't have any children of my own and they lived in the country. Our Peace Tea was a lovely turn out.

"We dressed the eldest one, Alf, in my friend's dress and put all this fruit on his head, 'cos he was tall. He was Carmen Miranda. The other one, Colin, we dressed as Aladdin. They had to parade in their fancy costumes. Alf had a good voice and sang 'When I love, I love.' He was so good. The judge said if he'd known he was a boy, he would have awarded him first prize! The boys really enjoyed it. There was some lovely music playing and it was a really lovely show."

CHAPTER
NINETEEN

Jews and Views

"I always thought what an awful thing it was how Hitler treated those poor Jews — it was wicked and they were the nicest people you could meet. They were lovely people. All those that I ever came across treated you fairly and were very generous. They ran a lot of businesses down our High Street.

Before the Second World War, my Dad's middle brother, Fred, used to work for the General Bus Company in Hoe Street — he used to drive the buses. When he was made redundant, he was out of work for some time and he had two boys. He couldn't get any work, so his wife turned him out and he went to London and strolled around for months and months — my Dad never knew where he was.

Well, what happened, he was going down Petticoat Lane and 'e never 'ad a penny in his pocket and it was pouring with rain. He was watching a Jew organise boots and shoes on his stall. He had been standing on the corner all the morning and I suppose he was tired and had got nowhere to sleep. At lunchtime, the Jew called over to him "Hello mate! Could you look after my stall for me? I'll trust yer. I'll be back in an hour."

So of course, Uncle Fred looked after the stall and, when the stallholder came back, he gave him some money and said 'Here you are mate. Go and get yourself a decent meal and then come back to help me,' which Uncle Fred did.

"And that man took 'im home, fed 'im, clothed 'im, found 'im a flat and found 'im some furniture. Uncle Fred worked for that man and lived in that flat right up until he died.

"The King and Queen in the Second World War were pretty good. She was always around people when they lost their homes; and the family decided to stay in London despite the bombs. I thought she was a lovely queen. About the best one we've ever 'ad, though the Queen Elizabeth we have now has done very well. Her mother thought a lot of George VI. He didn't seem to do a lot, but she used to support him, 'cos he was a nervous type and used to stutter a lot. Wonderful woman, she was. She done well in her lifetime.

"Regarding the abdication of Edward VIII, I thought the way he carried on with Wallis Simpson was awful. I mean — he knew what she was like. She'd already been married twice. And he abdicated because of her. He did what he thought was right, because he thought such a lot of her. But, if she thought she was going to be Queen, she was unlucky. I didn't have any sympathies with her.

"I think that going through what we did during the Second World War probably did make me a bit shell-shocked to a certain extent. I mean, we lost thousands and thousands of people and they never told us how many thousands were lost in and around London. All those who were lost in bombed houses and were never recovered — thousands of people. (*According to records, there were 301 fatalities and 2,833 people injured in Walthamstow during World War II. In London, 29,890 people lost their lives. Many more of course had their homes and possessions destroyed.*)

"But I think that my experiences during the war have made me a better person, 'cos it makes you realise what can happen and not to take anything for granted. And you had to make do with what you could get and make do and mend. We always tried to get a decent dinner, no matter what."

Part Four

1945–2003

CHAPTER
TWENTY

Pinks, Pails,
Bricks and Nails

Ethel had reached her mid 30s by the time the war ended. She and Joe remained childless throughout their married life. Though Ethel would have loved children, Joe did not want any: "His mother warned me that he didn't want children, but I told her 'Oh, I expect he'll have one with me, 'cos I love 'em!' In his latter years, he would say 'Oh, I wish I had a son to help me,' but I said 'Well, that's your fault!' My friend's breakdown after losing her baby shortly after birth during the Second World War — that's what turned my chap off from wanting children, I'm sure of that."

Instead, the couple directed their energies into trying to obtain building permission for their land in Doddinghurst, which Joe had earlier partly inherited from his parents: "Joe's Dad had been pensioned off in the 1920s — he had been a stoker for the electricity company — so he used his money to buy the land in Doddinghurst. It wasn't quite enough, so Joe would travel by motor bike once a month to Billericay to pay off the rest out of his own money.

"Joe's Dad would come to Doddinghurst now and again to escape for the weekend, and he would stay in the shed on the land. It used to cost him a shilling to travel by coach from Leytonstone to Brentwood. He would grow flowers on his plot — lovely pinks, which smelt like cloves — and would tie bunches of them onto a broomstick and sell them to the passengers on the coach on the way home to recoup his bus fare.

"Joe started up his own business after the war. He'd had a dispute with Ensign about a camera lens, so Joe said 'Thanks very much, I'm leaving.'

"He'd been doing some private repair work for Wallace Heaton in Bond Street, London, and also for Dolland and Aitchinson and Newcombes. He had a chat with another chap called Harry, who worked there, and the pair of them started up on their own. E.W. Repairs began in the back bedroom of our little flat in Walthamstow. Then we heard about an empty shop in Leytonstone from Joe's brother, so we put all the shelves in for storage and they set up in there. We hadn't yet started work on our house in Doddinghurst.

"I'd learnt some typing at evening classes, so I got a photography magazine, took down all the names and addresses of companies and sent out some letters. They got a lot of work. I did all the typing and mailing for them and all their accounts once a month, sitting up until the early hours. And I never got paid a penny — Joe said that I should do it for love!

"Every Saturday, after Wallace Heaton had telephoned me with a list of cameras, I would take the repaired items to Bond Street in a carrier bag. Although we had insurance for the cameras just in case they got stolen, I thought that the cameras would be more conspicuous if I'd taken them in a box.

"It took us five years to get planning permission for our house. I used to do all the writing and everything and I got on to the House of Commons and got the water laid on. Because of the war, building was very restricted. We finally obtained permission in 1950 and it took us about another ten years to complete the house, because we kept running out of money. They said that we could start building once we lived down here and had got permission to put on the water. By then we'd exchanged our rented flat in Roberts Road with a lady, who sold us her house in Higham Hill Road. We sold that for a profit and never had no mortgage. The money from that helped to fund some of the building of our house. Then we had to wait until we had a bit more money to finish it.

"Mum and Dad bought the bungalow next door and we lived in that for a few months until they moved in. We stored our furniture and then we lived in a hut on the land for two years while we built the first two rooms. We lived in those until we finished the rest of the house.

"Joe would work on the house during the day and on the cameras at night, sitting in the shed. When the building was completed, he gave up his camera work.

"Living in the hut was absolutely freezing during the winter months. We had no running water to start with (*although the couple had earlier received permission to put in a water main, they were unable to do so until*

111

their property had been built), so we used to have to carry it back from the large well up the lane in two pails swinging from a yoke across our shoulders. Then Joe managed to dig our own well, which is 32 feet deep. The water in that well has only ever dried up once. That was in the drought of 1976.

"One Sunday afternoon, the church bells were ringing when Timmy, the cat, frightened one of our chickens. It flew down the well and we had to pull it out with the bucket. We changed the words of the nursery rhyme 'Ding Dong Bell' to 'Ding dong bell, chicken's down the well; who put him in? A cat named Tim!'

"We eventually had the water laid on to the property on 24th June 1954. But we had a Jap engine generator for the electricity.

"In the shed, we had a little kitchenette at the back and a little put-you-up bed and then a little stove with a chimney sticking out over the brook. We used to take every drop of water out of the well and boil it all up for a bath. We had a screen that we'd put around us and my chap would sit in the armchair while I had my bath, then we used to pull the screen back, tip the water out in the brook and do it all over again. We both had a bath once a week.

"We did a good job building this house — just the two of us with our own hands, though someone did help for a while on the porch. The house has never moved in any way whatsoever. When we'd done the structure, I sat in the front room before we had any windows in, with a little iron block and straightened all

112

the bent nails out, 'cos we couldn't afford any new ones — it took me hours. Dad had showed me how to paper a room when I was 17, but I never told Joe in case he got me to paper all the walls too! Joe made a wooden block and we made all the bricks with sifted ash and cement. And my husband was a wonderful plasterer. There were papers for the brickwork, the woodwork, the roof and every part of the building that you finished had to be checked. I had a pile of papers.

"I only had the central heating put on in the 1990s, 'cos I couldn't keep getting on my hands and knees to make the fire every day."

CHAPTER
TWENTY-ONE

Pigs, Teeth and
Damson Jam

"We got the pigs roughly when we finished the house. Someone Joe knew had some, which he sold to us. Joe thought he could maybe make a living out of keeping animals on our two acres. We got more and more animals and in the end we kept 150 pigs, 100 laying hens, 100 fattening cockerels, 100 turkeys as well as rabbits, ducks, a goat, a dog and a tame pheasant called Joey. Joe had a boiled duck's egg every morning for 25 years.

"Just a few months after starting the piggery, we lost most of our stock to swine fever. Joe went with a friend to the market and bought six piglets there. Unfortunately, they had the fever and that infected the majority of the other pigs. When the inspector ordered them to be shot, I went next door to Mum and Dad's and put my fingers in my ears. We didn't get any compensation, but we re-stocked and fortunately were not affected by the foot and mouth outbreak during the 1960s.

"We used to send up to one dozen pigs off for slaughter at a time — depending on how many was

114

ready. The slaughter men allowed you what they called 'the pluck' — that was the lungs and the heart and all that — reasonably cheaply. And we had the pigs' heads as well. The pigs were weighed and we were sent how much they were worth. If we wanted a dead pig, we marked it with special ink. We used to hang the carcass in the doorway. Once the meat was cut up, I used to weigh it and mark who it was to be sold to — this was mostly at Christmas time. We used to get orders from Cousin Flo's firm. My friend, who taught me to drive, had the pig's head and she made brawn with it. It was beautiful. She used to bring us three of four pots of gorgeous brawn, which we ate with bread and butter, ham and tomatoes and all that. It was lovely.

'Two days before Christmas, Joe and I used to load up our van and drive to London to sell the meat. Once, we were returning to Doddinghurst at about three in the morning, when we were stopped by a policeman in Woodford Green. He asked what we had in the back of the van. We told him that there was a pig's head. He didn't believe us at first but after he'd checked us out, he let us go refusing our offer of the pig's head!

"I used to like the piglets, but once they went into the second sty to be fattened up, I didn't want to know them. I did, however, become very fond of one piglet, which I named Tina. Tina was the runt of a litter, so I kept her indoors for a while to feed her by hand. I even house-trained her. She used to love chocolate buttons, which she was often given by campers who came to buy eggs from us. We kept her for breeding.

115

"One sow, which was pregnant when we got her, had 24 piglets and was only able to feed 12 at a time, so I fed the others every two hours with dried milk and milk from my goat, Nan, who would only allow me to milk her. She always used to give me a kiss when I went to feed her. Cousin Les had come to see me on his birthday and was helping me with Nan. She thought that she would give him a kiss too. He thought that she was going to butt him, stepped backwards and fell into the brook! He was soaked!

"We brought our own boar a couple of years after starting our business. The boar usually served the sows twice a year. When close to giving birth, we put the sow into a furrowing crate, so that she didn't crush the piglets. We stayed with her while she was giving birth in case there were any complications. We lost very few piglets.

"Joe had a very clean mind and would never swear nor tell a dirty joke in front of me. He didn't think it right for a woman to see the boar and sow together, so I had to stand with my back to them after I'd helped him get the boar into the stall. When Joe said 'ready', I had to unbolt the door to let the boar out, but on one occasion, this big sow wanted to follow 'im. She caught Joe unawares and charged right between his legs, so the sow was facing one way and Joe the other. She rushed out of the stall, looking for the boar and poor Joe had his fingers scraped on the silver birch tree.

"My chap was six feet two, but that sow took 'im clean off his feet. It was the funniest thing I'd ever seen and I couldn't do anything for laughing, I just couldn't,

116

but he cried 'Don't just stand there, help me!' He eventually fell off just near the house, but he wasn't pleased at all, I can tell you!

"We fed the pigs with Tottenham Pudding (*the product of boiling lots of kitchen waste — including potato peelings and pea shells — from London*) — like a lump of black dough stuff, in a drum it was, we used to buy it in. The chickens loved it too. It made them lay lovely tasty eggs.

"We used to get the swill from a school in Brentwood, an old People's Home and from shops in the High Street — vegetables and peelings — and leftovers that farmers were unable to sell at market. We'd put it into a huge coal-fired boiler and boiled it all up, and then it went into a massive tank as big as my table. When cooked, we chopped it up and, while it was cooking, oh dear, did those pigs holler! They smelt it and loved it. And they didn't 'alf do well on it!

"When they (*The Board of Agriculture*) wouldn't let farmers make their own pigswill, because of the risk of disease, we used to buy in special dried food from the very old established firm, Marriage's of Chelmsford (*W. & H. Marriage & Sons Ltd. established in 1824*).

"When we had chickens before the war in the back garden, we gave them corn in the afternoons and middlings in the morning, nice and hot, to make them lay well.

"I used to pull 'em (*the chickens and turkeys*) standing out in the conservatory in the bitter cold, while Joe sat in front of the fire 'cos he didn't like the smell! A van used to come a few days before Christmas

117

to take the birds alive and, after they were killed and plucked, I had to pull them (*remove the giblets*). My fingers would turn blue with cold sometimes when the birds were frozen during the winter. The first time, I tried to pluck them myself and stayed out in the shed all night. But it was too much for me, so after that the dead birds were put into a steam machine to remove all the feathers. Good idea that was.

"All the dead poultry used to come back here. We would hang them in the shed and that's how they used to get frozen, if it was a cold night. I weighed 'em — some people wanted a small one, others a big one — and labelled 'em and charged half a crown for pulling 'em. Some of our customers didn't want their chicken or turkey pulled so I marked those to make sure that I got that right — 'Pulled' or 'Not pulled', see. We mostly received orders for birds at Christmas time.

"I would also load the basket of my bicycle with dead and skinned rabbits and take them into Brentwood to sell. I may not have always liked rearing these animals for slaughter, but it was our living. Joe wanted to be his own guvnor, so I just got on with it.

"But times were hard then. When people came in for a cup of tea, I worried about how far my quarter of tea was going to stretch. You know what I used to have to do when they'd all gone? I drained the teapots, put all the dregs on a tin tray, put the tray on the stove to dry out the leaves and use them again. I couldn't afford to buy another quarter of tea. That went on for years before I got my pension. I never 'ad no electric kettle or

118

anything. I always boiled up the kettle on the Aga stove, which I bought from Scotland for £37 in 1952.

"I had to make do with £2 a week. As well as a quarter of tea, I bought 2 lbs of sugar, as my chap always liked two teaspoons of sugar in his cup of tea and would not go without. I cooked myself a small dinner and gave him a larger one. Some days, I never had a dinner at all, but would always have a little one on a Sunday. I would have whatever I could find. Sometimes, it would just be a slice of bread and jam. I baked my own bread because it was cheaper, and used to make about 16 lbs of damson jam, which would last us all through the winter.

"When Joe and a friend used to collect the swill for the pigs at closing time in a horse and cart, the baker would sometimes fill up the egg basket with the cakes from his shop window that he hadn't sold that day, so I saved a bit of money then. I would pick out the best ones for us and the rest would be given to the pigs.

"I used to earn £1 for doing four hours cleaning at a shop, but packed that up when Mum got ill. After she died, I got another job cleaning for a lady, who had arthritis. I used to earn £1 for perming her hair too and I earned a little more from hairdressing for the neighbours. When we had the phone put on, I paid for all my own calls and used to save for one pair of stockings a month.

"We couldn't afford a lot, so when I needed to have my teeth out, 'cos I wanted a full set of dentures, a retired dentist came round one Sunday morning and pulled them out — after I'd had a local anaesthetic —

sitting at the kitchen table. As each one came out, he placed it in a bowl then tipped the whole lot down the brook! Afterwards, I cooked me roast dinner, chopped it up fine and ate the lot!! He did the same with Joe's teeth and Joe then went and mucked out the pigs!" (*The brook is unofficially named Elvin's Brook — not just because of the teeth episode, but because it is on land bought by Joe's father*).

One extremely sad incident that Ethel remembers vividly, occurred during the early 1960s while the couple were working on their smallholding: "I was in the garden one morning, when a man I knew who was out walking his dog, came round (Joe was seeing to the pigs). 'Ethel', he said looking worried, 'There's a man lying in the road. I know he's dead, because I've seen enough dead men during the First World War.' My next door neighbour was just about to take her two daughters to school and I didn't want them to see the body lying in the road, so I went indoors to fetch a blanket to cover him with. And they didn't see me, 'cos I dashed out of the way quick. The man was lying in the road beside a delivery van. He had died of natural causes. It was very cold and I believe he had had a heart attack. We phoned the police and a woman police officer came and arranged for the body to be taken away.

"I didn't know where the man lived, only where he worked, because of the van. I didn't hear any more and a fortnight went by, so I went into the shop and I asked the manager to give the man's wife a message: 'Please tell her that I was so sorry how her husband was found,

120

but that she could rest assured that he died in a nice quiet place and that the birds were singing.'

"We had to sell off the animals in the 1980s when we couldn't make much money out of them, because of having to buy in their food. It was a blessing in disguise really, 'cos it wasn't long afterwards that Joe became ill (*Joe contracted cancer and died in 1992*) and wouldn't have been able to look after them and I couldn't have done it on my own."

CHAPTER
TWENTY-TWO

Bombs, Buses and Dalmatian Bill

"Joe and I had a Dalmatian called Bill with us in Doddinghurst. He had been bombed out in Wanstead during the Second World War and had been running loose for about three weeks. He had been seen scavenging for food in dustbins and was so traumatised by the bombs that he wouldn't let anybody catch him. Eventually, Joe's friend, Jimmy, managed to get hold of him — by putting linseed oil on his hands (he said that a vicious dog shouldn't bite you if you did this). I made the dog some green trousers out of an old plaid skirt to stop him from licking his wounds after he had been treated at the PDSA Hospital. When the dog escaped again, we went round asking people if they had seen a Dalmatian with green trousers on!

"It was soon after the war, that Jimmy asked Joe and I if we would like to keep Bill, as he couldn't any longer. So we took him in and, as he had been so frightened of the bombs, we would bring him to Doddinghurst every Guy Fawkes Night, to escape the fireworks. There was a paper shop next to the ironmonger's in Walthamstow. One morning, I was walking Bill past the shops, when a man, parking his car close to the kerb, drove straight over a milk bottle. The bottle exploded, scattering glass everywhere. One piece just missed my lower leg, but another shard shot straight in Bill's right eye. There was blood everywhere. The car driver took him to the PDSA practice at Hoe Street, but the next day he was referred to their hospital at Woodford Green, where Doctor White advised that Nelson, as he called him (!), be kept in. He stayed for a fortnight. Fortunately, his eye was saved, but he did have a big white scar and lost some sight in that eye. I brought 'im home on the bus, which was a bit of consolation for 'im, because he loved buses. We found out that his original owner had been a bus driver.

"Every other Tuesday, I would take Bill by bus to visit a cousin of Joe's. The bus driver and conductress were husband and wife and we got to know them quite well.

"Once, we were a bit late and I thought that we'd missed the bus but, do you know, they waited for us as they said 'We couldn't leave without Bill!'

"It was because of his poor eyesight, that Bill grabbed a milkman's leg thinking it was a marrowbone! But the milkman was all right about it and in fact made a point of coming in to see 'im every day, he thought he was so lovely.

"It was probably Bill's eyesight that was to blame again when he grabbed a workman's ear. He didn't bite though — he was just a bit wary because of his sight and, when he realised who it was, he went and sat on

123

his lap! Bill loved children too, but once nicked a child's ice cream outside Woolworth's in Ilford High Street and I had to go and buy the child another one!

"Bill was about 15 when he died. It broke our hearts when that dog died. He was so intelligent and loving. We buried him in the front garden of our house in Doddinghurst."

CHAPTER
TWENTY-THREE

Collections, Councils and Clubs

"Dad and I started collecting for the PDSA before the last world war. We would often go out at five in the morning to sell flags. Dad would never hurt an animal. Before the war, my Dad used to do canvassing for Allied Supplies and Lipton's at Christmas time. We used to take a form round to the shops and say 'Come on, give us some money for the PDSA!' One year we collected £100 for the animals and they were so pleased with us that they sent us an invitation to tour the animal hospital at Woodford Green, where Bill had been treated. It was wonderful."

In 1939, after numerous fund-raising efforts including whist drives and selling books and other items from a trolley which she pushed from ward to ward, and collecting in the Walthamstow carnival for a few years, Ethel was elected a Life Governor of Connaught Hospital. For many years too, despite managing the smallholding and looking after her father (Edwin Turner died aged 91 in 1975), Ethel helped a lot in the parish council: "I used to go to the parish council meetings every month. They wanted to make me a parish councillor, but I couldn't have given it the commitment it deserved. I wouldn't have been able to do all the running around. I had too much to do at home and would have had to rely on other people to help me and I couldn't do that. They used to call me 'The Councillor'. I used to love it and learnt more about the village and other things than I would have done if I hadn't have gone out.

"I also helped run an Over 50s Club in Doddinghurst. I got involved when I saw an advertisement in the Brentwood Gazette and went along — without Joe. A Mr and Mrs Rushton ran the club. It started off in the large village hall in Doddinghurst then, as the number of members dropped, we moved into the small hall or priest house. We ended up eventually at the Rushtons' bungalow every Monday afternoon. When they got ill, I helped to look after Mrs Rushton and took over the running of the club for a couple of years until they died. They were lovely people.

"I joined the Horticultural Society as well. I made jam with me Dad. I won prizes — I've got all the show cards. I won first prize with my flowers. I had a big spray of carnations one year that I won with." (*In 2002, Ethel was made an Honorary Member of Doddinghurst Horticultural Society. At the time of writing, she is the oldest member.*)

CHAPTER
TWENTY-FOUR

Eating 'Ats and Highway Codes

After years of having to rely on her husband and father to drive her, Ethel passed her driving test at the third attempt aged 63 and continued to drive until she was 88: "I'd never even sat behind the wheel of a car before. Joe said that if I ever passed my driving test, he would eat his hat!

"A friend taught me for a while and Dad paid for me to have some lessons too. When I passed, I took off the 'L' plates and drove my friend home. Joe was mucking out the pigs when we got there. My friend and I had a glass of sherry each, then she went up to Joe and asked him 'So when are you going to eat yer 'at then?'

"Joe never congratulated me or nothing, but I used to drive him backwards and forwards to Harold Wood Hospital when he broke his arm and later, when he was very ill, took him to the doctor's surgery three times a week. He said to me one day, 'wasn't it lucky that you learnt to drive?' I replied 'Yes, and you were the one who didn't really want me to!'

"I failed my first test, because I spoke to the examiner when I wasn't supposed to. The second test I failed, because the examiner got his coat caught around the handbrake and I couldn't get away quick enough at the traffic lights. The night before my third test, I sat down and wrote out everything in the Highway Code word for word to make it sink in. During the test, the examiner hardly spoke to me at all until he asked me questions on the Highway Code. Afterwards he said 'That's strange — you've answered all those questions word for word!' We stopped by the station in Brentwood and he asked me to read out a car number plate nearby, then he said 'Congratulations and well done — you've passed with flying colours. I couldn't fault you on anything. I don't know why you haven't passed before.'

"A few years before I gave up driving though, I had a conviction concerning what I've since called 'The Bum Man.' Cousin Flo was paying me a visit. Well, she'd been down here for a week and we decided to go shopping in Brentwood. We were driving along, when Flo, seeing a man bending with his bottom towards the road, leant forward and yelled 'Look at that silly bloke sticking his backside out!' I couldn't see anything, because Flo was in the way, but heard someone shout, so I stopped and backed the car up. A woman told me that I'd just caught her husband on the bottom with the car and that she'd taken my number. By the time we reached home, there were two policemen on my doorstep. I couldn't prove that I hadn't hit the man, even though there was no mark on my car. I even had letters from my optician and doctor saying that I was okay to drive, but I was done for 'driving without due care and attention' and was fined and my license endorsed.

"I used to drive Dad's Morris Traveller. When he died, with the money he left me, I bought a Datsun. I decided it was time to call it a day when I had a minor accident and knocked someone's headlamp. The man drove me home. It was the last time I sat in the car."

CHAPTER
TWENTY-FIVE

Dutch Flowers and Scottish Lochs

When the last of the animals and poultry were sold off, the Elvins were able to go on their first holiday in years "with the couple of hundred pounds we had left and our savings." Ethel had never been abroad, but in April 1980, when she was 70, she went to Holland: "We travelled to the Hook of Holland by boat and the sea was ever so rough. During the crossing, which took several hours, we sat and played cards and drank tea, but loads of people were sick. I wasn't. The trip was organised through the church at Doddinghurst and we went to see all the flowers and the carnivals — there were motor bikes with Birds of Paradise all over them. I thought that the people were wonderful, the food marvellous and the markets were gorgeous — we had a lovely time. The hotel was really good. We came back by coach through Belgium and saw all the lovely lace.

"Joe and I also went to Calais for the day for our 40th wedding anniversary. On the coach to Dover, someone gave us a great big apple tart that they'd made for us and we didn't even realise that anyone knew that it was our anniversary.

"When we retired, we used to go to Norfolk by car to stay with friends and we went to Wales too and had quite a few holidays in Scotland — one year we had two holidays, in April and September. Four of us used to go — my friend Dorothy, who taught me to drive and her husband, Joe and I.

"Fort William was the first one in 1981. The Scottish scenery was gorgeous, especially around Loch Lomond, where out hotel was. I've never seen such lovely countryside in all my life — you don't want to go abroad, you want to go to Scotland — it's beautiful. At Loch Lomond, when you're up the top, you look down and you can see all the trees growing up the sides of the mountains. But if you're frightened of heights, you wouldn't like it. The coach is at the top and there's only a little road — oh, it's lovely! I thoroughly enjoyed it. The sun would be shining when we went up the mountain, but by the time we got to the top, it would be snowing.

"We took hot water in a flask and teabags with us, so we could have a cup of tea when we was out. We used to go from Brentwood and change coaches at Wembledy. We stopped overnight at Carlisle. We had trolleys for our luggage and our own seat numbers and we were insured too. Once, and old chap on board was taken ill. The coach driver took him to hospital and made sure he was all right. He was in hospital for a fortnight. Afterwards, the Eastern National gave him and his wife a fortnight's holiday and it never cost them a penny."

CHAPTER
TWENTY-SIX

Secrets and Reflections

Joe died from prostrate cancer in January 1992. He was 88 and Ethel had nursed him for two years at home as she had nursed her parents.

"Joe didn't want to go into hospital even though doctors advised it. So I made up beds for us downstairs, but hardly got any sleep. He did go into hospital at the very end and, just before he died, he told me what a wonderful wife I had been to him."

At the tender age of 87 and about five years after Joe's death, Ethel received a proposal of marriage from an old friend, who actually got down on his knees to ask for her hand: "I told him that I had a good many years with my hubby, was perfectly happy on my own and didn't want no changes. He took it all in good faith and there was no ill feeling between us, but I couldn't believe me ears. They couldn't believe it at the hairdresser's — 'Fancy, at your age, getting a proposal!' they said.

"I think that the secret to a long life is to work hard and to make the best of what you've got. Being jealous and envious of other people doesn't get you anywhere. You should also make sure that you eat all the right

132

foods — I love good old-fashioned wholesome food and lovely fruit and veg.

"I think that it also helps if you pick the right partner. Although Joe and I didn't always get on and sometimes, when he was in one of his moods and wouldn't talk to me, I did think about divorce, I thought 'Well, I'm his wife and he is my husband.' When we first got married, I thought that there was no one better. Mum said to me once after we were married 'You didn't get much when you were young and you're not gettin' much now!' I never had a row with Joe — I just used to keep quiet. But he was clean living (he said once 'I don't allow any rude jokes in my place!'), a good worker and didn't like wasting his money on drink. I'm not keen on people who drink. It breaks your home up and your money goes when you drink. We had a few laughs, especially when we went out together, but we never went out much when we came down 'ere, 'cos there was always too much to do.

"It's better to turn the other cheek, that's the way I've always been. I used to say to my friend, who wasn't very patient and who I used to work with during the war making bullets in the factory: 'Now look here Jean, don't do that. Count to ten.' That's what I generally did — count to ten. I was very patient, but I'm not always now.

"When I was a girl, mostly the men ruled the family and set the rules and boundaries and everyone had to abide by these, or face the consequences. Strict discipline had to be adhered to. In the main, because we were brought up to respect our elders, we very rarely strayed and always did as we were told. My father was very strict, but I believe that on the whole he was fair.

"Today, the younger generations do not have enough discipline, home rules and boundaries to abide by and so the respect for elders and their property is no longer there. Years ago, if we were told not to do something, we didn't do it. Today, if many youngsters are told the same thing, they do just the opposite as they think they know it all and that there will be no consequences for them. If anyone nowadays tries to check a young person in the street for something he or she is doing wrong — no matter what their age — they just get a lot of abuse or worse.

"I think that things have gone too far and respect, discipline and manners will never come back. I agree there has been a lot of progress with all sorts of things, to make life easier — health, travel, communication, general standards of living. If only we could get back respect, things would be better all round.

"The war years were very sad years, because you lost so many people you loved. But that was one thing about it — everyone pulled together and you always knew that you'd get help from somewhere. I've got lovely neighbours, but many people nowadays are just out for themselves. If you got bombed, someone would always come to help you. You could leave any doors open and you knew that no one would pinch anything. Nowadays, you've only got to blow your nose and someone comes in.

134

"To a certain extent, I suppose the world wars were experiences that I'm glad I went through, because it certainly made me think and I never take anything for granted.

"And I do think that they were right to have wanted to get rid of Saddam Hussein. But when you think to yourself of all those people who died, that's upsets you, don't it?

"I don't have any regrets about my life, but I would have liked to have become a proper hairdresser — I would have loved that. Now I just wish that I could walk better — I used to love walking. Still, mustn't grumble.

"There's a lot of people living in this age, who have gone through it all and your never forget it. I can talk, but I can't write. I can explain."

Also available in the ISIS Large Print Reminiscence series:

MY LUCKY LIFE
In War, Revolution, Peace and Diplomacy

Sir Sam Falle

With great modesty Sir Sam Falle shares his remarkable life in this exhilarating account of life in the Royal Navy and in Her Majesty's Foreign Service

A Jerseyman, Sir Sam Falle joined the Royal Navy and served in World War II. His ship was sunk by the Japanese and he spent three years as a POW. He was later awarded the DSC for "gallantry against overwhelming odds" while serving in HMS Encounter during her last action in the Java Sea. After the war he joined the Foreign Service and embarked on a diplomatic career.

Through his choice of career, Sam Falle has often found himself in the most extraordinary and unexpected situations. His memoirs make a most fascinating read.

ISBN 0–7531–9954–8 (hb)

DAISY, DAISY
A Grandmother's Journey Across America
on a Bicycle

Christian Miller

To pedal from the Atlantic to the Pacific? Surely too great a challenge to many but the formidable English grandmother, Christian Miller? She had no hesitation in volunteering her small folding bicycle, Daisy, and herself up for the challenge.

Daisy, Daisy is the marvelously entertaining story of her meeting with the United States of America and its people. Looking at America with a completely fresh eye, she is able to paint a picture of the countryside, the people and all things strange and wonderful that make up the America she befriended on her long journey. The stories she shares are witty, perceptive — and irresistible.

ISBN 0–7531–9950–5 (hb)

ISIS publish a wide range of books in large print, from fiction to biography. Any suggestions for books you would like to see in large print or audio are always welcome. Please send to the Editorial department at:

ISIS Publishing Ltd.
7 Centremead
Osney Mead
Oxford OX2 0ES
(01865) 250 333

A full list of titles is available free of charge from:
Ulverscroft large print books

(UK)
The Green
Bradgate Road, Anstey
Leicester LE7 7FU
Tel: (0116) 236 4325

(Australia)
P.O Box 953
Crows Nest
NSW 1585
Tel: (02) 9436 2622

(USA)
1881 Ridge Road
P.O Box 1230, West Seneca,
N.Y. 14224-1230
Tel: (716) 674 4270

(Canada)
P.O Box 80038
Burlington
Ontario L7L 6B1
Tel: (905) 637 8734

(New Zealand)
P.O Box 456
Feilding
Tel: (06) 323 6828

Details of **ISIS** complete and unabridged audio books are also available from these offices. Alternatively, contact your local library for details of their collection of **ISIS** large print and unabridged audio books.